Easter Monday

by Hal Corley

A Samuel French Acting Edition

New York Hollywood London Toronto

SAMUELFRENCH.COM

Copyright © 2009 by Hal Corley
ALL RIGHTS RESERVED

CAUTION: Professionals and amateurs are hereby warned that *EASTER MONDAY* is subject to a Licensing Fee. It is fully protected under the copyright laws of the United States of America, the British Commonwealth, including Canada, and all other countries of the Copyright Union. All rights, including professional, amateur, motion picture, recitation, lecturing, public reading, radio broadcasting, television and the rights of translation into foreign languages are strictly reserved. In its present form the play is dedicated to the reading public only.

The amateur live stage performance rights to *EASTER MONDAY* are controlled exclusively by Samuel French, Inc., and licensing arrangements and performance licenses must be secured well in advance of presentation. PLEASE NOTE that amateur Licensing Fees are set upon application in accordance with your producing circumstances. When applying for a licensing quotation and a performance license please give us the number of performances intended, dates of production, your seating capacity and admission fee. Licensing Fees are payable one week before the opening performance of the play to Samuel French, Inc., at 45 W. 25th Street, New York, NY 10010.

Licensing Fee of the required amount must be paid whether the play is presented for charity or gain and whether or not admission is charged.

Stock licensing fees quoted upon application to Samuel French, Inc.

For all other rights than those stipulated above, apply to: Barbara Hogenson Agency, Inc., 215 West 92nd Street, Suite 15G, New York, NY 10025.

Particular emphasis is laid on the question of amateur or professional readings, permission and terms for which must be secured in writing from Samuel French, Inc.

Copying from this book in whole or in part is strictly forbidden by law, and the right of performance is not transferable.

Whenever the play is produced the following notice must appear on all programs, printing and advertising for the play: "Produced by special arrangement with Samuel French, Inc."

Due authorship credit must be given on all programs, printing and advertising for the play.

ISBN 978-0-573-69696-1   Printed in U.S.A.   #29112

No one shall commit or authorize any act or omission by which the copyright of, or the right to copyright, this play may be impaired.

No one shall make any changes in this play for the purpose of production.

Publication of this play does not imply availability for performance. Both amateurs and professionals considering a production are strongly advised in their own interests to apply to Samuel French, Inc., for written permission before starting rehearsals, advertising, or booking a theatre.

No part of this book may be reproduced, stored in a retrieval system, or transmitted in any form, by any means, now known or yet to be invented, including mechanical, electronic, photocopying, recording, videotaping, or otherwise, without the prior written permission of the publisher.

MUSIC USE NOTE

Licensees are solely responsible for obtaining formal written permission from copyright owners to use copyrighted music in the performance of this play and are strongly cautioned to do so. If no such permission is obtained by the licensee, then the licensee must use only original music that the licensee owns and controls. Licensees are solely responsible and liable for all music clearances and shall indemnify the copyright owners of the play and their licensing agent, Samuel French, Inc., against any costs, expenses, losses and liabilities arising from the use of music by licensees.

IMPORTANT BILLING AND CREDIT REQUIREMENTS

All producers of *EASTER MONDAY* must give credit to the Author of the Play in all programs distributed in connection with performances of the Play, and in all instances in which the title of the Play appears for the purposes of advertising, publicizing or otherwise exploiting the Play and/or a production. The name of the Author *must* appear on a separate line on which no other name appears, immediately following the title and *must* appear in size of type not less than fifty percent of the size of the title type.

In addition the following credit *must* be given in all programs and publicity information distributed in association with this piece:

EASTER MONDAY
had its Professional Premiere at Pendragon Theatre
Saranac Lake, New York,
Robert Pettee, Managing Director

EASTER MONDAY had its world premiere at Pendragon Theatre, Saranac Lake, New York (Susan Neal, Artistic Director) on May 22, 2003. The production ran in repertory through August 27, and closed at the State University of New York, Potsdam, on September 26, 2003. The set was director- and company-created, set dressing coordinated by production stage manager Bonnie B. Brewer, with costumes by Rhiannon Marie Kramer, lighting and technical direction by Kristopher M. Kensinger, and sound by Samuel K. Shaw. The production was directed by Michael Montel with the following cast:

MACK ....Robert W. Pettee
BILLY... Jordan Glaski
ADELA...Molly Pietz

CHARACTERS

MACK – 55-ish; a radically sentimental, unapologetic Pollyanna; unselfconscious, devoid of vanity, he's alternately tender, prickly, impatient, cuddly, bullying, at times fiercely defensive and aggressively paternal.

BILLY – Mack's son, 20; attractively boyish, yet preternaturally world-weary; gentle, introspective and cautious, he has developed a short fuse, and though desperate to avoid confrontation, he can turn combative.

ADELA – Billy's birthmother; 35; unprepossessing, plain-spoken and intensely focused on whatever meager task is at hand; though decidedly meek, she's capable of standing up for the truth – and herself.

SETTING

A New York City apartment

TIME

Late March. Now, or a couple of years ago.

Which of us has looked into his father's heart?
Which of us is not forever a stranger and alone?

–Thomas Wolfe

ACT ONE

1.

(The living room of a rent-controlled apartment, the Upper West Side of Manhattan, New York. Yet this is not *a classically maintained pre-war with book-laden shelves and an eclectic mixture of new furnishings and heirlooms. This room's been repainted often, and brightly. The palate runs to deep blues, greens, purple. The last time the paint job wasn't quite completed, and a couple of the walls don't match. At first glance, one might think an eccentric illustrator lives here. The bookshelves are piled high with the family's accrued memorabilia, in particular a large collection of candles, figurines, small toys, etc. from various holidays [i.e. reindeer, ghosts, Cupids]. These items have been well cared for, and lovingly preserved, but are not consciously displayed with a collector's eye or the precious air of a retro gift shop. From the room's disarray, it's clear several domestic tasks are waiting: the dining table has mismatched breakfast dishes on one side, and a load of clean laundry piled high on the other. The apartment's currently being prepared for an impending move, but this seems a well-kept secret. There are a few boxes, but little actual packing has been accomplished.)*

(It's a chilly day in late March. Key in the door, intense voices off, then **MACK** *and* **BILLY** *enter.* **MACK**'s *55-ish,* **BILLY**'s *20.* **MACK** *wears one ice skate, one beat-up wingtip shoe, and holds a wrapped popcicle to his head.)*

BILLY. ...But it's *painless*. Flat on your back you ride, on a conveyor belt, through a, like, kitchen appliance kinda cabinet thingy. Like a big dishwasher in a restaurant. And they take infra-red snapshots of your whole skull. These colored slices of the brain come out looking sorta like –

MACK. – Jello parfaits. Seen 'em, Daddy keeps up. But they're not parfaits, they're tests, to make hospitals richer. Forget it, my brain's in one piece.

BILLY. You don't know! Will ya sit down? A brain doesn't even have, like, nerves to make you go ouch. Headaches hurt, sure, but headaches happen from the *inside* out, blood vessels shrinking too fast –

MACK. Somebody's been watchin' so-called news shows while I was napping.

BILLY. On one, they were digging 'round the back of the head of this woman who had epilepsy, and she was *awake*, talkin' about her horoscope.

MACK. "Watch out for greedy men with sharp objects."

BILLY. People can walk 'round normal for two days then, wham, they're on the pavement – Will you *rest!*

(Shoving **MACK** *into a chair.)*

I was scared you had, maybe, amnesia, you were so *nice* afterwards. We shoulda' 'least got the name of that girl who kicked you while ya were down.

MACK. To what, sue? Some tourist child from Venezuela? I ask you, what was somebody from the tropics doing on *ice*? 'Ever seen somebody from Caracas score big in the Winter Olympics?

BILLY. I dunno, you stopped letting me watch 'em –

MACK. Here she was in New York…making *do* with a thin, unzipped nylon jacket…and y'*know* she wanted to be anywheres else! Riding the Circle Line –

BILLY. – 52 degrees? Forget wind chill –

MACK. But didn't you notice? Earlier? When that blow-hard daddy laced up her wobbly feet, she was already miserable. I wanted to buy her hot cocoa and wipe her runny nose.

BILLY. Lemme see that head wound. Keep the popcicle on. I'll get frozen peas.

MACK. We don't eat peas since Mommy.

BILLY. Stop *fidgeting* so much!

(He starts unlacing **MACK**'s *other skate.)*

MACK. Your hands. They're shakin' terrible. Billy? *Billy.* It's not like what happened to Mommy. Hear me – ?

BILLY. – Well, I *know.*

MACK. Mommy didn't know what hit her –

BILLY. Be *still.*

MACK. – Here one minute, gone the – *Daddy* just gotta little noggin bump –

BILLY. – Okay, *o-kay!* Jeesh!

MACK. Doesn't help, it almost bein' the same time a' year. As Mommy's –

BILLY. – Will ya just pull your foot out? Do it fast, I'll bring ya a treat.

MACK. Ahhh! To wiggle my piggies again! Bring us some of those blue corn chips. I'm almost used to the color. And a glass of milk. Whole.

BILLY. Whole's soured. I dunno why we were even skating.

MACK. Closes this week, the rink. We only 'been twice all year. Weatherman's having fits about warm winds coming. "Warm winds blowing in good times." Who says? Who started this hating winter *conspiracy*? We didn't have a foot of snow this year. Winter barely made an appearance. How many times 'we go sledding, you n'me?

BILLY. Maybe one.

MACK. Maybe none. Ruined by those do-gooders with their snow fences to protect a mound of crabgrass.

BILLY. 'Fore we finally move, I'm gonna give my 'flyer to Stevie down on two.

MACK. No you're not, neither. They got *fine* sledding hills where we're going.

(touching his head wound)

MACK. *(cont.)* That kid who kicked me, she was maybe eleven. Had on lipstick. Why? That awful daddy, standing around smokin' his gold-tipped cigarettes. How do little girls get treated in South America? Think they have any fun?

BILLY. Venezuela isn't, like, the third world –

MACK. Really? Someday, I gotta start reading the newspaper again. No I don't. What a sad trip to our town she's having. When *I* first visited New York, way before we'd moved to Red Bank, by the way…

BILLY. Here we go.

MACK. No we *don't* go. You haven't heard this part. Ma'd saved some money for once, and managed a real vacation before we moved to that dump in Trenton. We took a train that had white tablecloths in the dining car. Checked into the Biltmore. The elevator man there took me under his wing and –

BILLY. – and showed ya where to buy a magic kit, in the hotel gift shop –

MACK. – and taught me what a Blue Plate Special was.

BILLY. Yeah? Plate you spin on top 'a stick?

MACK. The coffee shop's featured meal of the day. Meat loaf, chicken pot pie. In the shop's window, food was glued to a actual blue plate. The elevator man sang *"It Was Fascination, I Know,"* and the whole visit, whenever I saw him, he had a individual box of Chicklet gum for me and called me Mack The Knife. I did my magic act on him and he pretended he was tricked, and drew a map to get Ma and me to the Empire State Building. That girl from Venezuela, she got a elevator man like I had to look out for her on her trip to the Big Apple?

(**BILLY** *nervously nibbles some of the chips. He moves something that* **MACK** *has placed next to his computer, straightens his desk a bit.*)

BILLY. You *gotta* pack for Red Bank today. Still a buncha Mommy's, like, sit-around-home clothes and old pajamas we never got rid of –

MACK. 'Nother time.

BILLY. Daddy! Look at this place! We only got five weeks left, 'til –

MACK. – Not *today*.

(Wobbly MACK teeters a bit. Concerned, BILLY studies MACK's condition again:)

BILLY. When that girl kicked ya, I kinda did think…'bout Mommy. I wondered, did she have one-zillionth of a second to, like…like say… *'bye?* Inside her head? Don't they say the brain doesn't go that quick – ?

MACK. "They say, they say." If there's anybody I hate, it's "they." That's something we don't need to take to Red Bank. Television, and every know-it-all "they" on it. We'll have so much to do, we won't turn it on, ever.

BILLY. There musta' been…'least a flash…when Mommy thought about something. You n'me? Without her?

MACK. You know Mommy. Probably just remembered some darn thing on her desk 'shouldn't have been left there the whole long holiday weekend.

(beat; this hangs in the air)

Here it is, almost time to decorate for it again.

BILLY. Easter this year, we'll be all packed.

MACK. So, it will still happen here. How can winter be done already? There's nothing to help the transition. No… Easter…*carols*. You can't turn on FM radio and hear something 'puts ya in a mood. There's no *second* when you suddenly go, "awwww…. *Easter*." 'Cause something 'cuts *deep*. Second week of December, you're sick to death of western singers rockin' round silver trees, then bam, you hear, I dunno – "The Little Drummer Boy" – one time, and you're *connected*. There's no Easter "Little Drummer Boy."

BILLY. Yeah, hear that drummer kid, ya picture, like, 'black sky, big star, kings on camels. "Swaddling clothes," whatever they are, animals, like, keeping that baby warm in a barn. Easter's about an empty tomb.

MACK. Yeah, yeah, but not *only*. Not to a grinnin' little boy who's found a pale pink egg in his bedroom slipper, just as the sun comes up. *(looking toward shelves)* Hey–

BILLY. Just sit still a minute, will ya?

MACK. – You think we still got a copy of "Here Comes Peter Cottontail" 'round here somewhere? *Not* the Danny Kaye, the *original*. Gene Autry, 1950!

BILLY. You kiddin'? Probably a *couple*. You need more ice for your head.

MACK. Hey, where 'you putting those skates? Not in a box!

BILLY. Oh yeah, skatin' season's over.

MACK. But it was good when we first got there today. I could feel my cheeks get rosy. They played some old song with lots of harmony, I coulda' closed my eyes, *Mamie* was still First Lady. And boy, there was no stopping you. First coupla years we skated, you always held my hand, got ticked if I let you go a second. Then, third grade, no more with the hand. Cut me to the quick.

BILLY. I held onto you today, half a time around.

MACK. The sun came out, it got slushy, they put on that awful stuff that rhymes and has no tune. Who can skate to *noise?*

BILLY. Not you. I shoulda' kept on, maybe you wouldn't have that shiner.

MACK. When I slipped…and knew I was, y'know, goin' down…I only thought…about you. How…how if Daddy…ever got…laid up –

BILLY. – Forget that! *Nothing's* gonna happen to *you!*

MACK. *(beat)* It's a oven in here. I hate this time of year. Everybody *outside* all of a sudden. Sidewalks full, people elbowing each another like they're rushing to a sale at Gimbel's.

BILLY. *Gimbel's?*

MACK. I wanna stand up on a bench and shout "go home!"

(BILLY steals a glance at his computer, maybe momentarily resting his hand on it. He moves to the window. A strategy, to cheer MACK:)

BILLY. Clouding up again. Look at those fools, 'left home with no coats. Still winter, Daddy. Cozy, huh?

(no reaction)

Hey! I'll make us a great big pot of firehouse chili. I got down a buncha board games to pack up. We can eat chili and play Chinese Checkers.

MACK. Don't even *think* of packing the games so early. And wait! Don't turn on the lamps yet –

BILLY. – I know, I know, let the sun set first. I still like it better that way, too.

(He sits behind his computer, turns on the screen. Covert, he takes the focus off this private activity by distracting MACK:)

You used to drag my tail to the park on Saturdays like this. When the carousel first started up again? It *sure* was going strong today. 'Least the calliope always sounds the same, huh? – Will ya go put some fresh ice on that head a'yours?

(MACK takes the popcicle off his head, gives it a lick.)

Go *on*, now! 'Fore you swell up more n' turn purple!

(MACK starts off. BILLY drums his fingers, visibly anxious to go online, but waiting till MACK is gone. Reflective MACK turns back:)

MACK. When you don't actually *ride* that merry-go-round… when you don't wait in line to buy a long string of tickets…or pick out your horse, and give him a name… that calliope's just background noise.

(As MACK finally shuffles off to the kitchen, BILLY exhales, drained from the care and attention above. He can finally steal a moment, and fully boot up his computer. MACK continues to ruminate aloud:)

MACK. *(off)* Off in the distance, it's one of the saddest sounds there is.

*(In the darkened room, **BILLY**'s face is illuminated by the computer screen. As the programmed "Windows" theme chimes its automated musical greeting, **BILLY**'s instantly visibly engaged by this contact with another world. To him this music is anything but sad. His expression changes; he looks at the screen intensely, then begins typing. Lights fade on him, alone, momentarily activated and fully connected.)*

2.

(Sounds of a pouring rain, thunder. After midnight, a few days later. **BILLY**'s *just come home, sits in a chair. His hair and clothes are wringing wet. He glances over at his desk and the computer, contemplates getting up – Then, he hears a noise, tenses slightly, and flops back in the chair.* **MACK** *enters in a flannel robe, carrying a much handled game.)*

MACK. Scrabble and grilled cheese sandwiches?

BILLY. I can't breathe in that shop. Too many smells. The toner from the machine. Then all the perfume and cologne from the people who come in. Door opens, whoosh. Like those pages in magazines with the little sample things glued shut. You have to rip out the page just to get through the rest of the magazine. Then, the other guys there. After their breaks, they come back inside, and when a guy who's just smoked stands near a heated-up copier 'been on for hours, there's one hot stinky mix a'fumes. Then if you add pizza breath or something with, like, curry powder, this foul cloud forms right in the middle of the shop. I gotta walk through it, holding my breath. Spices n'chemicals, garlic and cigarettes. I dream about that stench. Wake up, it's on the pillow case where my head was. I walked out on Amsterdam tonight, rain came. Everybody ran, papers over their heads. I stood there, gettin' soaked, just to get the stink off me.

MACK. I found your Culinary Institute application. Ya haven't even started to fill it out, and there's a deadline y'know. And, uh, I noticed a locked drawer by your computer, there.

BILLY. Smells real strong like vinegar in here.

MACK. Never been locked before.

BILLY. You 'been dying *eggs*?

MACK. Me? I don't know how to dye eggs.

BILLY. If you do it too soon, they rot –

MACK. The Easter Rabbit's the person in charge of eggs. I thought this drawer was just stuck. I tugged, I kicked. But no, she's locked all right.

BILLY. Daddy, I can't make egg salad outta week-old eggs, we'll just throw it out –

MACK. – Don't *ruin* the one nice thing about this time of year.

(beat)

'There a key to this thing? Did Mommy have the key?

BILLY. I dunno, Mommy knew you hated locks.

MACK. You spend hours bangin' away on that computer Mommy bought ya. Print up stuff from it sometimes, too. I hear. You lock up papers you print up in that drawer?

BILLY. Just recipes. I read 'em to get, like, ideas. Go back to bed. Rain puts normal people to sleep, you wake up like a vampire.

MACK. Who 'you writing to on your computer? Some nice young ladies?

BILLY. *(evasive; new tactic:)* There's a doorman job open on 81st.

MACK. Why lock up your letters in a drawer?

BILLY. A doorman gets to spend maybe half his time outside.

MACK. *Doorm* – Frankie Silva? Fourth grade? Remember the tragedy 'happened to his daddy? I tried to keep it from you, but oh no, your Mommy blabbed how he was gunned down in cold whatever. Afterwards, you woke up screamin' for weeks. Every time, *who* got *up* with ya? And played tick-tack-toe 'til ya got sleepy? Not Mommy with her big mouth.

BILLY. Hasn't been a doorman even *hurt* in, like, ten years.

MACK. You're gonna be a chef, use your talents. Doormen get varicose veins and become big red-faced alcoholics. Carry little airplane bottles of vodka in their breast pockets, always sucking on wintergreen Lifesavers to cover up.

BILLY. Plenty of chefs are *serious* drunks –

MACK. – You're not commutin' from Redbank to be a darned *doorman!* What's *in* that locked drawer!?

(BILLY crosses to it.)

BILLY. It's – heeey! – already open! You went in?

MACK. I just jiggled it.

BILLY. You go in my pants pockets for the key?

MACK. You don't need to keep stuff hidden from Daddy. I don't care if you wanna meet young ladies out there in the computer airways.

BILLY. You read stuff?

MACK. I couldn't help but see names. New pen pal? Like the one in Australia –

BILLY. – No. This lady isn't a pen pal.

MACK. She got something to do with cooking? Pretty little souchef, maybe? Who is she? Is she Jewish? 'That why it's secret? *Billy*?!

(Tense BILLY is silent, then makes a decision:)

BILLY. She's her. *Her.* 'Lady I was born from. I found her. My mother.

MACK. *(beat; fear rising)* Impossible. That person didn't wanna ever be found.

BILLY. You pay thirty-five dollars, they find anybody.

MACK. "They?" What "they" is this, now? How?

BILLY. I had the file Mommy kept. I give 'em my birth date, the city I was born in. They did all the foot work.

MACK. No.

BILLY. Yep –

MACK. She's a fraud. You 'been taken.

BILLY. *No*, I was born in Arlington, Virginia. She lives in Virginia, near where they got that flame for John Kennedy that doesn't go out, and works in Washington, DC. It's *her*.

MACK. Why 'you go and do this now?

BILLY. Why not? Like, what else I got goin'? Copy shop, sleep, copy shop, pack.

MACK. 'That all you think we do – ?

BILLY. Now's as good a time as any. They got me her whole name, I wrote to her after Christmas, she finally wrote back a month ago, right there online.

MACK. You did this that far back without me knowin'?! What kinda things this person say to you?

BILLY. 'First, I thought she was a teacher. 'Cause when I typed all in small letters, she asked if I'd finished school. I didn't tell her *that* whole story. She seemed kinda worried, 'maybe I didn't know sentences start with capitals. I told her it's too much trouble to hit a shift key. I wrote her a "Ha!" But she didn't send back a "Ha." 'Guess she's what you'd call "a woman of few words." Mommy always said I could someday meet her.

MACK. Mommy was smart as a whip but said a ton of stupid things, and Mommy's not here to face *this*! Computers! I hate 'em even more than televisions – !

BILLY. Daddy, calm dow –

MACK. Oh, I heard all *about* digging up these women. Next thing ya know, she'll be your so-called new best friend, *wanting* things –

BILLY. Naw, naw, she lives five hundred miles away –

MACK. *(over)* – For you to come down! So she can parade you 'round. I'm so stupid – I saw the name tonight, I'd forgotten it – ! My big fear was that you'd started obsessing on another Jewish girl. I didn't want your heart broke again, I got so shaky, my hands started sweating.

BILLY. Your hands sweat if ya see a newspaper headline. With *good* news.

MACK. So, she's got our address and number now? And will be phoning regular?

BILLY. She's not like that.

MACK. Yet. *Yet!*

BILLY. Daddy, will ya just turn in? You're still all shook up from gettin' your head beat at the ice rink.

MACK. – I'm "shook" from *this*! You're writing her every day now?

BILLY. We're down to sending, like, two sentence messages.

MACK. Ah, *strategy*! She's playing hard to get. Lying in wait for you to ask her if she *needs* anything.

BILLY. Daddy, go back to bed. Take a swig a'cough medicine to *relax* you. I'll come in and read *Twenty-One Balloons* out loud to you for a change.

MACK. Why? I'll never sleep, now.

(sound of distant thunder)

BILLY. 'You ever actually meet her yourself? Way back, when?

MACK. Mommy wanted to. Me, I didn't even want to see her picture. Luckily, she didn't care to meet us. 'She tell you?

BILLY. She stays way clear of all that stuff.

(watching **MACK** *with concern:)*

I won't check the computer tonight. Come on, now, hit the old sack. Tomorrow's a big day. Red Bank, remember? First time in months. We'll buy a "Welcome" mat for our new house…hit the Woolworths to check out their Easter decorations. That'll make you feel better.

MACK. 'Night we brought you home, it was October. Leaves had turned, but it was so sticky. 'Cause it was Columbus Day, we had to come back from Washington on the slow train, and the air conditionin' was on the fritz, and there weren't enough seats. So I stood part of the way, and my whole shirt got sopping wet. Then black, from this dirt n'soot coming in the window. Mommy's whirlin' dervish mind started thinking about all the darn *troubles* on the horizon. Would this dark little place still be big enough for us all. Could we send ya to PS 87. Would her job at the bank be there when she was ready to go back – Yeah, well, she was ready in a month. All her worrying gave me a migraine, so I sent her off to the dining car. While Mommy was buyin' herself *two* so-called light beers and a ham sandwich, I changed my first diaper. I guess nobody on that slow train had ever seen a man touch a diaper before, 'cause everybody was whisperin' and pointing and smiling. When somebody pulled out their camera and took a picture of me, a coupla people clapped. I felt famous, like I'd just found the Lindbergh baby.

(beat)

And…relieved. For the first time, I knew what I was born to do.

BILLY. Honest, Daddy. We're already kinda outta conversation. We won't be writin' each other much more.

(Suddenly guilt-ridden, his allegiances torn, **BILLY** *stares at* **MACK**…*)*

Daddy? I'm sure.

(…then back at the computer. Fade down.)

3.

(The next late afternoon. Agitated **MACK** *and* **BILLY** *burst in, carrying shopping bags.)*

BILLY. Calm down, calm *down!* Kids 'been breaking into deserted houses for a goof since *cavemen* times. They just smoked a few cigarettes, drank wine coolers –

MACK. Urinating in our fireplace?! Would've never happened before. Not *there.*

BILLY. It's like a dog raisin' his leg on a *hydrant.* 'Place has been sitting *empty* so long, kids just, like, claim it. Ammonia got rid of the pee-pee, we can paint over the graffiti.

MACK. Words like that were never *spoken* in Red Bank. Let alone written –

BILLY. Once we're in, nobody'll come near. Like the cops said.

MACK. *Them!* Those aren't homegrown Red Bank boys-in-blue. That one with a tattoo looked at me funny.

BILLY. 'Cause when you cry, you get this kinda *yodel* sound in your voice –

MACK. He wasn't welcoming, you could just tell: He hopes we never move there.

BILLY. How 'you get *that* from what he said? "Get new glass for the window. Change your lock. Mow the lawn." Just, like, normal advice –

MACK. That cocky attitude, it's not Red Bank. But these things are symptoms. The problem's bigger than juvenile delinquents and sarcastic police. The soul of that sweet town's being chased out – *drowned* out! – by those loud cars with the thumping stereos. You used to hear yourself *dream* there, just walking down West Broad Street.

BILLY. You take it personal. Like they put it on just to mess with your head.

MACK. You don't get it. Nobody would've wanted music that loud when I was a kid. Not there. You didn't bother people that way just 'cause it wasn't *nice.*

BILLY. Okay, but why'd you get all shook about the whatnot place goin' under? Stores come, stores go.

MACK. In that town, at this point in history, the closing of the Woolworths is a death sentence. I bought model airplanes there. My Lionel train track.

BILLY. So, we still got your old broken train. Somewhere…

MACK. And if next time I got clobbered harder, by a bigger ice skate, and ended up in a coma or dead, would you even keep my train?

BILLY. Don't you say that!

MACK. Would you throw all this out? Light a match to it, walk out, close the door, never look back?

BILLY. Don't you ever say somethin' crazy like that again!

*(Shaken **BILLY** unpacks some things they bought, then tries another tact to calm **MACK**:)*

'Least I got some useful stuff at that Goin' Outta Business sale. Right? This air filter runs about twenty here.

MACK. You already got air filters in your room. And I saw you buy that box of masks. You gonna be wearin' oxygen soon. A chef makes his living smelling aromas. You're always gettin' rid of 'em.

BILLY. So what. I saw *you* sneak off n'buy those old dusty Halloween candles. Ghost n'witch candles with the wicks missin'. Like we need more of that stuff? We just gotta pack it up anyway.

MACK. Come October, you'll be happy to see me put them out. Mark my words.

*(**BILLY** goes to the computer, goes online.)*

What's so important you gotta check your doohickey, there, first thing?

BILLY. Go have a snack. I got you vanilla wafers – 'old fashioned kind that don't have fat taken out. You can dip 'em, suck milk out 'way you like to. Set up a game for us. Scrabble always cheers ya up.

MACK. Whatcha' reading, there, that's so darn urgent? *Her?*
BILLY. Nothin' –

(**MACK** *swerves closer.*)

Just set up the Scrabble board. You can come up with "vandal" or "urinate," make yourself big points.

MACK. *Is* it *her?* Lemme see.

(**BILLY** *tries to turn off the screen.*)

BILLY. Daddy! Some things gotta be private!
MACK. *(reading)* She's comin' to New York. I knew it. I told you, she'll want something.
BILLY. She's here two days to see a Easter lily show at the 'Garden.
MACK. Ah, her *cover*. She's clever.
BILLY. I'll meet her at a coffee shop on 57th and Sixth and we'll be *done* with it.
MACK. *She* won't be done. She'll come in tattered hand-me-downs that smell like moth balls. She'll see that expensive watch I gotcha after you passed your test, her pupils'll turn into saucers. 57th street, oh boy, she'll pass some souvenir display in a tourist trap. Some Lady Liberty thermometer made in China you'll have to buy her –
BILLY. There ya go –
MACK. – That'll start her on a *roll*. She'll make you take her shoppin', so she can see our fine stores. Near some cosmetics counter that'll make you pass out from all the fumes, she'll get herself sprayed. You'll have to buy her four ounces of Elizabeth Taylor perfume for a hundred n'twenty-five dollars, and that'll just be the beginning –
BILLY. No *way* –
MACK. – 'She know your Mommy's dead?
BILLY. Well, *yeah* –
MACK. – Uh-huh, she spies a *opening*.
BILLY. She just wants to see my *face* –

MACK. Ha!

BILLY. – nothin' more. So, will ya just get over it?!

MACK. She *thinks* she can *hook* ya, play actin' being Mommy, now.

BILLY. Daddy, I'm gonna be twenty.

MACK. You didn't shave 'til you were sixteen n'a half –

BILLY. You said I'd cut myself –

MACK. – She'll *see*. Sense you're not completely *formed* yet. So she can still have *influence*. Sorry, but no. No. You can't meet her.

(**BILLY** *just stares. His Waterloo:*)

BILLY. *I'm* sorry, but I'm *gonna*. Mommy woulda wanted me to.

MACK. Mommy was the one secretly terrified we'd get a letter from the girl's oily lawyer. Some October afternoon, 'crisp zing in the air, stores all strung with orange and black, you'd be decidin' who to be for the big night, we'd come home and find papers in our mailbox announcin' she wanted ya back.

BILLY. She doesn't want me back. I'm a grown up.

MACK. No, no, *no*, if you must see her, *I* gotta go with you –

BILLY. Wha – 'You *crazy* – ?!

MACK. – So I can figure out what she's *after*. You'll get all tongue-tied. Start flippin' open the coffee creamer, tearin' up the placemat edge 'til it's fringe. Rolling your napkin between your palms 'til you've made a skinny paper rope. You know how ya do, arrangin' it on the table into a Casper the ghost shape or somethin'. *I'll* pay attention.

BILLY. Nope –

MACK. Hone in on what's up her sleeve.

BILLY. I'm going by myself.

MACK. I'll sit across! Give ya the *signal*, so you don't completely humiliate yourself in front of her.

BILLY. Didn't you hear me? I'm meetin' her *alone*.

MACK. – No! You'll try not to, but you'll start pickin' your nose. You know you will. Sometimes, you still put boogers in your –

BILLY. *(over)* Shut up, now, Daddy! Just shut up! You're not coming, and that's that! Don't say any more about it.

MACK. *(beat)* You'll be defenseless without me.

BILLY. I'll take my chances.

(He turns off his computer, picks up **MACK**'s *purchases from Woolworths, tosses them to him.* **MACK** *catches them, flopping backward in a chair. Lights down. Music: a scratchy record plays an uptempo song from the 50s, Rosemary Clooney or Jo Stafford.* Lights up on:)*

---

*See Music Use Note on Page 3.

4.

(Morning. Good Friday. Energized MACK's busily sorting through things from the shelves, putting some in one box, some in another. He wears a flannel nightshirt, wool socks. BILLY drags in from the bedroom, yawning, wearing faded pajamas. Suspicious, BILLY takes the needle off the record. Sniffs the air.)

BILLY. You 'been baking. This early? How come?

MACK. The raw weather inspired me to fire up our oven. Look outside. Old Man Winter ain't giving up the fight yet. Spring'll have to wait.

(BILLY looks down at:)

Recognize? From scratch I made them: Jelly Surprise with two cupsa' Wheaties, from the Betty Crocker book Ma gave Mommy. Have one. Concord Grape's in some, peach in others. I baked 'em when I was class parent, remember?

BILLY. Packing, too? Wow.

MACK. You done somethin' with your framed fifth grade school picture? Send it to that pen pal you had in New Zealand?

BILLY. Who cares, now.

MACK. I said, "Send the wallet size." But no, you musta mailed him the big one, along with our only Polaroid of the diorama you did of the Berlin Wall coming down. I loved that diorama. You used a doll for the president. What was his name?

BILLY. Ronald Reagan.

MACK. 'Pen pal.

BILLY. Francis Waterbury. Christchurch, New Zealand. He thought you were a soldier 'got hurt in some war, 'cause you didn't work.

MACK. That boy had so-called emotional problems.

BILLY. Why 'you wanna dig up my fifth grade picture now?

MACK. So you can show *her* of course. She's gotta realize she's walking *into* something built on rock. *Here*: I packed you a whole shoebox of *evidence*.

BILLY. I don't wanna haveta' *carry* stuff; and we only got an hour –

MACK. Ha! This lady'll plant herself in that coffee shop till you stand up to go. She'll want to hear how ya grew into what you are. So you offer proof: The three hundred dollar stroller. Hanging your stocking for Santa – the one Daddy sewed ya from scratch. First day of second grade when you got stung by a yellow jacket and I had to carry you to St. Luke's on my back, so you wouldn't die of anaphylactic shock. The Halloween I made ya into Zorro, again, a costume from scratch. Naturally, you in eighth grade, 'only boy on the East Coast enterin' the Pillsbury Bake-off.

BILLY. *No.*

MACK. Yes. Show every one. Don't let her thumb through 'em and slam them down. Even if she cries – *sobs* – all over her tuna melt, for the *effect*, you tell her a story with each. Embellish.

BILLY. *(thumbs through the stack)* Weird. Every picture's just *us*. Almost none of Mommy.

MACK. Mommy loved playin' photographer.

BILLY. You just always handed her the camera. And got me to plaster on the same goofy grin.

MACK. Goofy my foot, you 'been one happy kid. That joyful expression's the real McCoy. Look at you at the Bake-off. Holdin' up your prized Manhattan Biscuits. Cream cheese, your secret ingredi – Don't put that back! Be proud of the Bake-off!

(BILLY turns his back; covert: He leaves picture.)

Also, wear this tonight.

BILLY. You bought me new clothes – ?

MACK. She'll judge us both if you show up a slob in dungarees.

BILLY. She won't care how I dre –

MACK. I *care*.

(He hands him a muffin and a glass of milk. **BILLY** *takes it, then holds, surveys the room.)*

Eat up while ya dress for work. Go on. Don't get jelly on those khakis.

BILLY. Wait – whatcha been *up* to? Looks like…you 'been taking things *outta* cartons we already packed. Putting 'em back on shelves?

MACK. A few supplies. We're not moving for weeks yet.

BILLY. Good Friday tonight. I know you. Bet you're gonna pop popcorn, n'watch "Easter Parade" on Channel Eleven…

MACK. If I can stand the parade of obscene commercials.

BILLY. How 'bout something, like, *bold*. Invite that new neighbor lady in to watch with you. One in 7G? Wears the same *perfume* as *Mommy*…

MACK. We're movin', why get cozy with her now?

BILLY. In the elevator, she told me she's still got no cable –

MACK. She starts conversations nobody wants to have with her.

BILLY. Be nice, 'least she doesn't smoke or wear a Walkman.

MACK. A do-gooder trying to yank our carriage horses off our streets. 'Last civilized thing we got left. Tried to get me to sign a petition. Talked about how the animals freeze and sweat. Their lives are torture, she says. They're *horses*, I says.

(He glances around the room:)

I'll wait up, maybe bake you n'me something seasonal. Coconut bunny cupcakes.

BILLY. *(with fresh eyes:)* Y'know Daddy…you spend a lotta time by yourself –

MACK. Well I won't in Red Bank. Our neighbors *there* will become lifelong *friends*. Now, will ya go now, and put on your clothes so I can see how bad a mistake I made?

(**BILLY** *shuffles off with the bag, a half a muffin. Pensive* **MACK** *starts to play his record again, but stops, rifles through a box, finds an aged, pastel "Happy Easter" sign. He takes it out, holds it up. He starts to fret, calling off:*)

MACK. Remember, this…person you're meeting from Virginia, she's here for facts, so you give her exactly what she's come to hear. You know how…*tentative* you can get. *Billy – ?*

BILLY. *(off) Huh – ?*

MACK. Are you listening to me?!

BILLY. *(off)* Do I ever gotta *choice*?!

MACK. Let her see how well you recall everything you and me did *together* – she'll be judging your daddy, oh boy, make no mistake. Don't dwell on that copy shop. Talk about how temporary it is, 'til you take off as a chef. 'Course leave out the whole high school thing – but otherwise, toot your own horn. You got one to toot. Nobody knows more than your proud daddy.

(**BILLY** *returns finishing a big bite of muffin, wearing the new clothes. It's an ensemble in bright colors.* **MACK** *beams.*)

BILLY. I look about twelve.

MACK. Twelve's a good age. You almost won the Pillsbury at twelve.

(**MACK** *takes charge*)

Keep it clean. Roll up these sleeves at that stinky shop, and be careful not to slosh toner or sit in cigarette ashes. On second thought. You'll get wrinkled. No, take these, changin' *later*, at the shop –

BILLY. No! Lemme go; I'm gonna be late –

MACK. – Your hair should be shorter, but all the good barbers are Italian and Good Friday, they'll be confessin'. So at least carry a comb for once.

(smoothing down his hair)

And a coffee shop's no good. You take her to a real restaurant.

*(**BILLY**'s frustration continues to mount. **MACK** goes to a steel box.)*

BILLY. Okay. Then let me use my credit card. Give it to me.

MACK. I cut up all our credit cards.

BILLY. Cut – ?! *Mommy* gave me that, when I turned seventeen! For a present –

MACK. Some darned presents she picked. Credit cards, computers.

(counting from a thick stack of cash:).

– You buy this woman a roast duck with a flaming boysenberry gravy, and show off when you read the menu. *Here.* A hundred smackers oughta hold her. Hide it from that little miniature U.N. you work with.

(examining him critically)

And run cold water on your pale face 'couple minutes before you leave work, so it gets pinker. Or she'll think I never fed you a green vegetable.

*(**BILLY** again tries to pull away.)*

And you show her all your pictures – and…and maybe take along your menu collection! You brag for once. 'Hear me? Billy?

BILLY. I'll tell boring stories about every wonderful second I've had on planet earth since I got kidnapped by you!

*(As **BILLY** finally tears away, he inadvertently shoves **MACK** hard.)*

Stop *fiddlin'* with me!

*(A moment that's never quite happened before. Palpable tension between them. He scoops up the pictures, throws them in a backpack, starts out. **MACK** panics:)*

MACK. Hey. Billy – ?

*(**MACK** crosses over, takes his face in his hands, plants a kiss on his cheek. **BILLY** dutifully but sincerely does the same to him. Then goes.)*

Remember, don't you eat some big gooey sweet thing –

(calls out to hall:)

MACK. *(cont.)* – With *her!*

(desperate suddenly:)

You be sure n'save room for a treat with your daddy!

*(But **BILLY**'s gone. Silence. **MACK** is suddenly overwhelmingly alone. He picks up the dropped picture of the Pillsbury Bake-Off, stares at it. Then puts it down, starts to hang up the "Happy Easter" picture. Fade.)*

5.

(That night, shortly after nine. Dark room. Key in the lock, then the front door is thrown open:)

BILLY. *Ta-daaa!*

*(Light spills in from the vestibule beyond the front door. **ADELA** enters past **BILLY**. She's a pretty, fragile but nononsense woman of indeterminate age. No jewelry or discernable frills. She wears a raincoat over a monochromatic pant suit and flat walking shoes. Her accent is indigenous to the Washington, DC area, but not typically drawl-laden "Southern.")*

(In half-light, we see that faded pastel-colored cardboard rabbits and tulips adorn the walls.)

*(An attentive host, **BILLY** crosses the darkened room, and turns on a lamp. The bulb blows.)*

BILLY. Darn *it*.

(calling off)

Daddy?! 'So dark in here. *As* usual.

ADELA. A left-on light can be a real fire hazard. I believe that's why we only have fluorescents in our Federal offices.

*(**BILLY** illuminates another lamp.)*

BILLY. Take off your rain coat. Daaaad-*dy!? 'You hooooome?!*

(thrown)

Can't believe it. He's out.

ADELA. He don't go out?

BILLY. Not too much lately. I said, take off your coat.

ADELA. 'He sick?

BILLY. He had a head injury 'coupla days ago.

ADELA. *Head* inj –

BILLY. *(over)* – It's nothin'. Thought he was gonna watch "Easter Parade" tonight.

ADELA. From y'all's window? Y'all hold a parade for that up here?

BILLY. It's a movie. Daddy'll only watch stuff on TV that wasn't made to be *on* the TV to begin with.

ADELA. I knew this clerk-typist when I was just a GS-6 at the Commerce Department who came down with that mental illness where you're 'fraid to go to the grocery store and everything. When she stopped even raising her venetian blinds –

BILLY. He's not that way –

ADELA. – her brother from North Carolina come to get her and take her back home –

BILLY. If you meet him: Daddy's, like, *different*, but –

ADELA. – Even though you never hear 'bout that many people getting cured of their mental illnesses in the mountains of North Carolina.

BILLY. Daddy's not mental. Daddy fell at the ice rink, that's all.

(holding up the doggie bag)

Hungry yet? You barely nibbled on your pork chop a la whatever.

ADELA. That black herb in my gravy made my eyes tear up.

BILLY. I knew a coffee shop woulda' been better –

ADELA. I know it cost twenty-two ninety-five, plus a dollar seventy-five for my ginger ale, and Mr. Doyle tells me folks in New York leave great big tips –

BILLY. Forget about it.

ADELA. – but like I said, I just get suspicious of spices I never met before.

BILLY. So! What can I get ya?

ADELA. Just water'd be good.

BILLY. Just ol' H2 – ? Me, too. Never get enough. Ice cold, right outta the tap.

ADELA. I don't drink water from pipes when I go to new towns. Ever since this Fall Foliage Bus Tour I took, I found out you can get a sour stomach 'cause you're not used to the bugs in a strange place's plumbin'. Got anything in bottles?

BILLY. Ice tea, maybe.

(As he goes off to get it, she looks around at the toys, etc. He calls in.)

I *said* take off your coat! Stay awhile!

ADELA. 'Your daddy run hisself a day care center in here?

BILLY. *(off)* A *what?*

(He enters with her drink; she gestures toward the toy-laden book cases.)

ADELA. These colored sisters in my apartment building ran 'em a illegal day care and got arrested or fined or in some kinda trouble with the law. There'd been a'lotsa coming and going and what-have-you. People'd hear all these toddlers crying through their door when they left for work and everything. We'd all thought they just had some kinda big family reunion that wouldn't quit –

BILLY. Well, *sure.* Y'know –

ADELA. – Then, this homosexual man 'cross the hall took to spying on 'em regular and saw the gals tossing hefty bags fulla disposable diapers in the basement. It stunk up the trash room somethin' terrible, so I couldn't blame him for turning them in.

BILLY. Whoa.

ADELA. But the colored sisters had always seemed nice enough to me.

BILLY. I didn't wear disposable diapers. Daddy didn't believe in 'em –

ADELA. 'Paper kind make lots more sense to me.

BILLY. – 'Washed cloth ones. We still got a bunch in a trunk somewheres we'll use for rags someday –

ADELA. I eat on paper plates pretty much 'year round. A built-in Hotpoint dishwasher come with my new apartment, but I only had it on one time to get the newspaper stink off all m'pots n'pans after I moved in. You sure got lotsa toys.

BILLY. I do, don't I? Interesting, like, how quickly ya noticed –

ADELA. Can't miss 'em. Y'all have neighbor children in to play?

BILLY. We don't know most neighbors.

ADELA. Me neither. The colored sisters used to say howdy-do back if I spoke first, but otherwise kept to 'emselves. Prob'ly on account of turnin' out to be criminals. Those iddy-biddy kinda toys sure collect a'lotsa dust.

BILLY. Want me to take a few down? Show you some of my all-time favorites?

ADELA. Don't go to no trouble.

BILLY. Hey, it's what you're here for, right?

ADELA. At m'office, I put in an employee suggestion about us having too many empty shelves, as part of Uncle Sam's ongoing efforts to eliminate waste –

BILLY. – You must wanna, like, fill in a few of my "blanks," and my *home* tells –

ADELA. *(over)* – I got a letter that's suitable for framing from the head of our agency along with a fifty dollar cash award. They finally sent some folks from GSA to tear the shelves down. I spent the money on a new humidifier so's my nose wouldn't dry up in the winter months.

BILLY. Uh-huh. Growing up, I was very, like, creative. Can you tell? 'Used to treat all my toys more like puppets. Daddy used to let me stay home from school, for what he called "recharge days – "

ADELA. You got sick a lot?

BILLY. No, no – *anyway*, since he wouldn't let me turn on TV, I'd hold, like, these action figure Olympics, and give 'em tiny medals made outta gum foil. Really, it'd be easy to bring down a few of my Gold Medal Winners, in case you're kinda interested in seein' exactly what I played with.

ADELA. I see 'em fine from right here. I won a doll in a contest.

BILLY. Yeah? Me, I useta' –

ADELA. 'Grown-up lady doll.

BILLY. – secretly play the lottery –

ADELA. The doll come with homemade clothes and what-have-you.

BILLY. Nice. I used to want to win *cash*, so I could buy my own television –

ADELA. This woman's club raffled it off, all the women in the club made the doll outfits. There was a miniature mink coat, and different uniforms, so's you could make believe the doll had different jobs I s'pose. Nurse. Bank Teller. Cone Dipper at the Baskin Robbins –

BILLY. Cute –

ADELA. – I kept her in her silver astronaut uniform most of the time, 'cause I could just wipe that one off with a wet paper towel.

BILLY. You a kid when ya got her?

ADELA. No, grown up. They sold raffle tickets at work. Which is against U.S. Government personnel regs. Along with betting on the Redskins and buyin' each other Christmas and birthday presents in excess of ten dollars, by the way. But since I bought the ticket during m'lunch, and was standing at least a hundred feet from U.S. Government property, I didn't actually do nothing against the regs.

BILLY. Who's this Reg?

ADELA. Reg-u-*la*tions.

BILLY. Uh-huh –

ADELA. – Mr. Doyle, Mr. Warren Doyle, my supervi –

BILLY. – Mr. Warren *Patterson* Doyle, 'guy who took a chance when he picked you from a list for your G girl job, right?

ADELA. My *GS-8* Career Conditional Secretary Position.

BILLY. You mentioned this Doyle 'coupla dozen times during dinner.

ADELA. Guess I can't help it. Mr. Doyle's the best supervisor I ever had the privilege of working for. Did I tell you he's a handicapped gentlemen, who refuses to use the special parkin' places –

BILLY. And walks with braces without even gettin' outta breath.

ADELA. Well, he put out what he called a real strongly-worded memorandum on the inappropriate use of government facilities for personal business. 'Specially gambling. I'd never want to let him down, bein' seen with a raffle ticket –

BILLY. 'You give her a name?

(**ADELA** *stares, baffled.*)

The doll you won.

ADELA. A *name?*

BILLY. Oh, sure, I name all my stuffed animals, action figures –

ADELA. – No. Just "doll." I did keep doll right there –

BILLY. Look up there –

ADELA. – in my bedroom. 'Least, for a while –

BILLY. That guy, way up there? He's named Gunga Din, and that one, Hannibal –

ADELA. – since I'd never won nothing before. But she took up so much space on my dressing table and kinda stood out, not really matching nuthin' in my apartment, so I finally let her go.

BILLY. Gave her to some poor kid?

ADELA. I don't really know no children, 'cept my niece, and she's a tomboy 'says she wants to be a wrestler on the TV when she grows up.

BILLY. Well! This –

ADELA. – So I just propped the doll up against the door of the colored sisters who run the illegal day ca –

BILLY. – Is! The *actual* home! Where I grew up!

ADELA. Those two locks on the door do the job, keep y'all safe?

BILLY. Absolutely. I gotta ask –

ADELA. Y'all have smoke alarms? You change the batteries when you're 'posed to? I always change when I Spring Forward and Fall Back. "Spring forward, fall ba – "

BILLY. – Sure, sure! Listen! Is this what you, like, *expected*? How you…pictured where I was, you know, raised?

ADELA. Can't say's I expected anything in particular. At supper you said both y'all are moving?

BILLY. To Red Bank, New Jersey. Sweet little kinda old fashioned town on the Navasink River.

ADELA. 'That safer?

BILLY. I told you, *this* is safe –

ADELA. – Your Mama got run over by a subway train near here.

BILLY. By accident. It wasn't a regular subway train. It was a special yellow car 'only run nights to pick up garbage and make repairs. Her briefcase was open, 'transit police thought she musta' been, like, *preoccupied*, and just backed up too far and slipped. Daddy tried to get the engineer driving the train sent to Rikers Island, but the transit board said he hadn't done anything wrong. Third rail's what actually killed her.

ADELA. I thought nice people up here mostly ride around in taxi cabs.

BILLY. Mommy was nice; Mommy said cabs were a waste of money.

ADELA. Now your daddy's got hisself a head injury?

BILLY. It's got nothing to do with us living in New York –

ADELA. – 'You see your Mama dead?

(beat; **BILLY** *'s thrown)*

In her coffin? All laid out? I saw mine and sure wished I hadn't.

BILLY. Daddy and me didn't want a funeral. Nobody woulda' come but, like, her office people n'us. Red Bank's where Daddy lived a while when he was a boy. We bought this house about a year ago with Mommy's insurance.

ADELA. A year? Musta' needed some fresh paint or what-have-you.

BILLY. Daddy's just not *quite* ready to make the move. Wanna see a picture?

(He takes a framed one down from a shelf.)

ADELA. Why, it's a...old house.

BILLY. Exactly. Built seventy-five years ago.

ADELA. Musta' got it cheap, then.

BILLY. No, no, it's what they call a classic. High ceilings –

ADELA. – I go for your newer model townhomes. I put some money in Certificates of Deposit at the Northern Virginia Savings so's I can someday purchase a townhome of my own. I want to live someplace where nobody else has spent a single night. Where nothin's been inside the cabinets, nobody's taken a bath or flushed the what-have-you's.

BILLY. Well you'll never find *that* –

ADELA. – Yes I will, too.

BILLY. Sorry, but *no* –

ADELA. Yessir, I plan on it.

BILLY. Come *on*, guys who built 'em have to at least run water in the sinks to wash their dirty hands! And use the toilets! *This* house, in Red Bank, has mostly got all new plumbing –

ADELA. What's it smell like inside? Some grandmama's old tea rose perfume? Or maybe like old dirty mongrel dog?

BILLY. So strong smells bother you, too?

ADELA. I read in an old Readers Digest your taste buds and nose go first when you get older. I wish mine'd give out now. I can't stand the stink 'comes from just *regular* things.

BILLY. *Me* neith – !

ADELA. *(over)* – People say, "Umm, getcha a good whiff of this new Avon hand cream, just like real apricots." But I just hold my breath and pretend. Real apricots.

Who'd want their hand to smell like some apricot? When I get a cold and my nose gets stuffy, to me it's a vacation.

(looking at framed pictures)

ADELA. *(cont.)* How's come you don't have a picture of your high school graduation day up there?

BILLY. What.

ADELA. Where is it? You in your cap and gown?

BILLY. I...I dunno. I just didn't –

ADELA. You graduated, didn't you?

BILLY. *(paralyzed:)* I showed you plenty 'other pictures. Wouldn't you like to see my room?

ADELA. Why?

BILLY. 'Cause it's got all my more...grown up stuff.

(**ADELA** *nervously checks her watch.*)

It's not even that – It's because it's where I go. Where I spend a lotta my time by myself these days.

ADELA. That's okay, but I would just like to wash up after that cab ride. The way he turned corners on the red lights kinda gave me the willies. I held on tight to that strap, and ever since, I can't stop thinkin' how dirty my hand's gotta be.

(She exits. **BILLY** *slams something down.* **MACK** *enters, his cheeks pink, dressed in a heavy fur-lined parka, boots. He carries grocery bags, throws them on the couch.)*

MACK. Aren't we back early.

BILLY. Where 'you been?

MACK. Enjoying this last icy gasp of winter, of course. Flurries have begun, a significant accumulation's expected, on Good Friday, yet. In two days, we'll have bunny tracks in a foot of white stuff!

(BILLY slams something down.)

Ahhhhh. *I* get it. So Herself couldn't be bothered to stick around too long, eh?

BILLY. She stuck 'round, like it was a sentence.

MACK. Um-hm. Daddy won't be cruel and say "Told ya so – "

BILLY. She's still around.

MACK. *(racing to window)* – It *is* starting to *stick!*

BILLY. Not just New York. Here.

MACK. – *Here?*

BILLY. She's washin' her taxi-cabby hand off, right there in our bathroom. Like a idiot, I brought her back.

MACK. What the heck 'she want, now? William?! Tell me!

BILLY. – Nothing! But to hear herself jabber!

(ADELA enters. Mutual sizing up:)

MACK. Well, well, well. Hello, Dear.

ADELA. You Bill's Daddy?

(He grabs her hand, deadeyes her:)

MACK. When my boy was four years old, he told everyone – checkout clerks, strangers on the street – who his best friend in the whole world is. Know who that person was? Who that person still is?

ADELA. His pen pal in New Zealand?

MACK. Yours truly, Dear.

BILLY. Dear's name is Adela.

MACK. *(watching BILLY closely)* I know the nice lady's identity. But if I didn't know better, I'd swear *you* had an alcoholic beverage at supper –

BILLY. Adela's a G-8 Girl who wins awards for stoppin' waste.

ADELA. *GS*-8.

MACK. And I'm the award-winning Daddy.

(He takes off his coat, he has various treasured "World's Best Dad" ribbons and other buttons given him by BILLY, stuck to his sweater.)

BILLY. *(almost a warning)* Sure ya don't wanna at least stick your head in my room for a minute? So we can talk by *ourselves*? This is my last offer.

ADELA. No thank you. I 'spose I walked past it. One with the little animals piled up?

MACK. Santa Claus has been very, very good to my boy.

ADELA. Betcha don't get no sun to speak of, with that ugly old building right outside.

BILLY. I can see a sliver a'sky. There's nothing wrong with my room.

ADELA. I got me a air cleaner pretty much like yours, only a later model. The filters to the SX-4000 series are real hard to find –

BILLY. Uh-oh.

ADELA. – so I get 'em from the company direct using their 800 number or what-have-you.

BILLY. Aren't you smart.

ADELA. You're 'posed to change 'em every 90 days, but I do it once a month.

BILLY. Do it in your office and win another award or have some *regs* changed.

(wheeling on **MACK***)*

– Why'd you go out? You never go out at night anymore.

MACK. Had to find some much needed staples for our larder. You know me, I'm not scared of a little weather.

ADELA. A clerk-typist back when I was at the Commerce Department came down with that mental illness where you're 'fraid to go to the groc –

BILLY. You told me, and I told you, my dad isn't sick with that *particular* mental illness.

*(***MACK** *watches, savoring this sudden tension between* **BILLY** *and* **ADELA.***)*

MACK. 'Course not. I used to love late night shopping. Remember when I couldn't sleep in the summer? I used to get you outta your bed and take us to the air conditioned all-night Food Emporium, you still in your 'jamers. We'd fill up a whole cart with cereal and crackers we had coupons for, cake mixes we'd never tried.

The store'd be empty, we had it to ourselves, remember? Well, tonight, the old Emporium was *packed.* 'Had this electricity in the air. After that depressing taste of early summer, people were *happily* back in mittens and ear muffs. Turning to one another in the aisles, sharin' treasured soup recipes, buying up all these foods they thought they were through with 'til All Saints Day. When I said I was making beef tips and noodles, the crowd at the meat counter got dinner ideas...

(BILLY takes ADELA's doggie bag, heaves it in the trash. She jumps. MACK starts unpacking. Ovaltine, minature marshmallows. ADELA watches, concerned:)

ADELA. I always check expiration dates on package foods 'fore I buy em. If oatmeal or what-have-you isn't fresh, it don't taste the same. Takes on whatever's nearby –

MACK. Luckily, Mr. Quaker Oats still puts his product in that reassuring cardboard cylinder, which Billy and I always saved to make castles from.

BILLY. *(over)* – Adela was just goin', right? She got to be a real "nice" tourist tonight, take a taxicab ride. See where I live, kind of. Here's your raincoat.

ADELA. I shoulda brung a heavy winter coat up here.

BILLY. You shoulda' brung a lot. You can get a cab out there on Amsterdam. Better move it.

ADELA. You said it's snowin' out?

MACK. We got some old umbrellas right over here I never threw out. Even halfway working, they do the trick.

(She pulls out a pastel one with an animal handle, starts to put it back.)

BILLY. That one was mine. At least *look* at it. It's got a whole story 'bout the time I stole it at a street festival, and Daddy made me track down the vendor to pay him, all in pennies. But you wouldn't wanna hear.

ADELA. Will the taxicab driver know how t'get to where I'm staying?

BILLY. If you only tell him what he needs. Leave out Mr. Doyle's favorite leather chair and the black sisters' bogus daycare. Just say which hotel you're at, and ya got about a seventy-five percent chance of gettin' there in one piece.

ADELA. Are most taxicabs really safe? For a gal who's by herself?

BILLY. You could be brave n'ride our subway. Go on, you'll have tales to tell Mr. Warren Patterson Doyle. I dare ya. You'll *probably* make it. You won't end up laid out in a pine box.

MACK. *(startled)* William.

(**BILLY** *erratically moves to* **MACK**'s *phonograph, puts on an old scratchy recording. He turns his back on* **ADELA**. **ADELA** *slowly begins to bundle up.* **MACK** *has no choice but to turn to her:)*

MACK. Uh, travelling all alone, Dear?

ADELA. Employee association tour. Thirty people's the limit. I always put my deposit down the first day the flyer come out, even if I change my mind.

(**BILLY** *turns up the volume.*)

MACK. By yourself in a crowd, as it were. – William? Turn that down, hm?

ADELA. I got a roommate back in the hotel.

MACK. A friend to see our sights with.

ADELA. No, 'cost more to get a room by y'self. I'm with a gal who come up here to buy herself some summer clothes at some fancy store y'all have. Only twenty-eight years of age and already divorced.

(**BILLY** *turns the music even louder;* **ADELA** *talks to* **MACK** *over it.*)

Last night she smoked cigarettes in the bathroom after lights out. I was gonna report her to the hotel, seeing as how we're on a non-smoking floor, and all our towels smelled smoky. But she'd already picked a fight about how I'd sat on her dress, so I didn't want her to come after me. I didn't even know it *was* a dress. She didn't put it on no hanger. Stretched out on m'bed, 'looked like a nightgown or what-have-you.

MACK. Well, Easter finery isn't what is *used* to be – William, the record's a wee bit – ?

(**BILLY** *scratches the needle over the record, darts to the window.*)

BILLY. 'Stopped snowing! So *you* can *go.* You don't even need the broken umbrella.

(**MACK** *adjusts/retapes some of his sagging decorations.* **ADELA** *takes them in:*)

ADELA. Can't say's I care much about Easter. I don't go to church no more –

BILLY. *(over)* Bye *bye.*

MACK. – Well, Easter's not just for your pious types. We had Easter long before the man with the beard and sandals y'know –

BILLY. *She* doesn't *care.*

MACK. – Easter's a *ancient* festival, celebratin' this Saxon goddess and this kid of hers, Eastre. Y'see, Dear, the Christian missionaries came along, saw these pagan customs, and decided to steal 'em and stick 'em *onto* the story of Himself on his cross. The heathens joined in, so no one would persecute 'em for *being* heathens, get it?

BILLY. You'll get a cab before all the movies in the neighborhood let out –

MACK. So when the missionaries saw this old festival, celebratin' the start of spring, it worked out just perfect for their little *cause.* They *lifted* the whole shebang, even the word Easter –

BILLY. *(almost pushing* **ADELA***)* Now's the time to make a *run* for it –

ADELA. – But what about…the *bunny?*

MACK. Y'mean, when did he begin hopping?

ADELA. Who was it, 'made him up?

MACK. *(sacrilege)* He's not made up!

BILLY. 'Longer ya wait, more likely it is to start snowing again.

MACK. The bunny made appearances as early as that Saxon festival –

BILLY. *(over)* – Hear what I'm saying? Time to scram –

MACK. *(over)* …which means The Big Fuzzy White Guy must've hopped into pagan huts and mud-floored shacks before Jesus was ever a gleam in his Father's eye.

ADELA. There was a Easter Rabbit before *Christ?*

MACK. Yes indeedy there was –

BILLY. Gimme a break. Don't keep her here!

MACK. Y'know, Easter never really caught *on* on our shores 'til after the Civil War. I'm not sayin' Mr. Rabbit hadn't been comin' earlier, it's just nobody noticed –

BILLY. *Daddy!*

MACK. – Imagine what those folks tryin' to deal with slavery problems must've thought of those pretty eggs appearin' from nowhere.

BILLY. What*ever*!

(He throws open the front door, stands by it.)

MACK. William, *where* are the manners I drilled into you –

BILLY. Why 'you running on like this?! 'Bout the Easter Rabbit? To her?

MACK. It's a history lesson, like we used to have when I had to take over where your teachers left *off* –

BILLY. You just wanna show off! You don't care about her! You wished she hadn't come! And it turns out, she came for nothin'! We coulda skipped eating, and just shook hands on the street!

(No one speaks, then:)

ADELA. I musta' hurt the boy's feelings, not finishing my pork chop at supper. I don't eat in fancy restaurants. 'Never know what to pick. And when we first sat down, there was no spit in my mouth for a long while. And it was a good thing you were doing the talking about your work fixing those photocopy machines, 'cause even though Mr. Doyle has told me I'll get more used to speaking to people if I just start tellin' whatever pops into my head, tonight I didn't have nothing to say.

BILLY. Nothing to ask. You had plenty to blab about you, but not a thing to ask about me!

ADELA. He told me when you meet somebody you don't know how to talk to, you should write down questions way before. I did put some on cards –

(opening purse)

I wrote questions out, things I thought I was 'posed to ask a boy. But I'm not good at memorizing, and I forgot I even had the cards.

BILLY. What about what you *wanted* to know? Didn't you just have, like, a million questions 'bout me, way down inside you?

ADELA. I didn't.

BILLY. How come?!

ADELA. 'Just didn't.

BILLY. Why not?

(He grabs the note cards from her hand.)

You didn't even take out your lame notecards. What was on 'em? "You like the Redskins, as a team?" "Were you a Eagle Scout?" "Your Daddy vote for Republicans regular?" Those aren't *questions*. You had to have real ones! Buried in your GS-whatever brain! What's wrong with you? Even coming back here, there was nothing in this room you wanted to ask me about!

ADELA. I did want to see one thing: 'Picture of you, in your cap and gown. When I signed all them papers to turn the baby over, the lawyers said, "Don't think of it as a little helpless baby. Picture it all grown up, holding its high school diploma. Then you'll know you did the right thing for it."

BILLY. *It*?!

ADELA. That's the one thing 'stuck in my head, 'cause I myself never got to graduate. I thought you might have a copy, to give me.

BILLY. "It" got no copy, 'cause "it" never graduated *either*. "It" hadta' get a GED, like some drop-out *retard*, and work in a xerox shop. Now ya know. So you can just turn around and go home and throw away your cards.

ADELA. At the hotel, I said to m'self, "Remember to look close…remember to memorize the boy's face, for when you get back to Virginia." But…when I tried…I couldn't take in the whole thing. Only one part at a time. Piece of your forehead, by your eye brow, or one red spot like a chigger bite, by your ear, or a chipped place on your tooth. It was a jigsaw puzzle, and I couldn't see nothin' but pieces.

BILLY. When you looked…in my eyes, 'same color as *yours*… didn't…didn't you feel something else? *Anything?!*

ADELA. *(blurt) Trapped.*

(beat)

I just wanted to be home again. On my new sofa 'just got delivered from Penney's, watching my Friday night shows. I didn't want to be in no New York restaurant or anywhere but in my house, all by myself.

BILLY. Then go! GO! And be by yourself *now!*

*(**BILLY** pulls back, looks toward the hall, silently waiting for her to leave. She stares at him, then glances around the room, at all the toys and childhood trappings)*

The sooner the better!

*(She slowly goes. **BILLY** slams the door shut again. **MACK** unpacks a large holiday cake from the bakery of a grocery store. He holds it up to **BILLY**, smiles nervously.)*

MACK. I'd just better make sure she gets herself a taxi. Then! You and I! Will dive into that cake! Just *us.* Hang on.

*(As **MACK** exits, **BILLY** picks up the cake, throws it at the back of the door, hard. **MACK** bursts back in, startled.*

*(**BILLY** reaches up, rips down **MACK**'s Easter decorations with one strong yank. Blackout.)*

End of Act One

ACT TWO

6.

(The next day. Sunlight pours in. **BILLY** *enters from his room, his hair disheveled, clothes slept-in. He spies a faded Coney Island prize stuffed bear, dressed in the once-worn clothes of a toddler.* **BILLY** *moves toward it as* **MACK** *enters from the kitchen, whistling "Easter Parade." Upbeat* **MACK** *wears summer pajamas, and on a tray carries two brightly colored children's mugs and the bag of miniature marshmallows. Before he can greet him,* **BILLY** *erratically wheels on him, accusingly:)*

BILLY. Whatya doin' now?

MACK. Ovaltine! *Somebody* got up, *just* in ti –

BILLY. *(over)* – No, no, with that bear there. Wearin' my old clothes?

MACK. He was *hiding* from us, in the hall closet. You're the one 'put these clothes on him, remember? When you were nine? First summer all your buddies went to camp?

BILLY. You wouldn't let me go.

MACK. 'Cause you were terrified.

BILLY. You said I'd get stung by a hornet and with no hospital 'round I'd die in the middle of some forest.

MACK. Well, you could've. And did ya miss *out* on anything? Counselors teachin' ya how to roll your own marijuana cigarettes?

BILLY. It's somethin' I don't know how to do.

*(***MACK*** busily continues his preparations, dumping marshmallows into the cups.)*

MACK. Nobody goes to those boot camps in Maine except uppity kids whose lazy parents don't wanna take time to raise 'em. They all end up at psychiatrists the rest of their twisted lives 'cause of the insanity and degradation that went *on* there. You may've been heartbroken you were in the city alone, for a day or two. But later, we always had more fun –

BILLY. On the playground with nothin' but four and five-year-olds.

MACK. – Who reminded you of the sweet part of yourself you didn't have to say 'bye to. *Ever.* That summer you made me take out all your old baby pictures, and all the baby clothes –

BILLY. You never would throw out.

MACK. – and I was happy to, I was, just to show you what you'd looked like.

BILLY. – You can throw the clothes out now. And the bear.

(*He checks his watch.* **MACK** *adds more marshmallows, nudges a mug closer.*)

MACK. Don't worry. I *called*. The store.

BILLY. Woolworths?

MACK. Your so-called shop. Even though they tried to get rid of me with that awful call waiting, Daddy *handled it*. Though it's a miracle they understo –

BILLY. (*over*) Handled what? What'd you go n'do now?

MACK. 'Said you're sick, can't make it in. There's such a thing as bein' *too* dependable. Mommy was, and what the heck did all her dedication get her?

BILLY. A big salary, to support all 'us.

(**MACK** *starts to amend this, then lets it drop, moving on:*)

MACK. In every job, there's always something called "personal days."

BILLY. In a eight-buck-a-hour photocopy shop?

MACK. What you gain from a quiet morning 'home always helps you.

BILLY. Quiet. Right.

MACK. Like when Daddy usedta let you play hookie every now and then.

BILLY. To keep you company.

MACK. When ya needed to recharge your batteries. A family tradition. My Ma kept me home whenever she got ready to job-hunt and move us again, just to remind me there's more to life than the three R's and always bein' someplace people *expect* you to be. Look outside. Snow's melted. Spring's in our air.

BILLY. Then why aren't you slittin' your wrists or something?

MACK. I'm resigned. That last burst of Frosty the Snowman's icy breath will have to satisfy Daddy till next autumn. When we're cozy in our new home, fire roaring, pot of vegetable soup on the stove, Apple Brown Betty in the oven, good smells floatin' through every room.

*(surveying untouched mug, **BILLY**'s hangover:)*

If you want, I can make you tea instead. We still got that fancy English Breakfast stuff Mommy used to sip Saturday mornings. 'Specially after those drunken office shindigs she claimed she hadta' go to.

*(**BILLY** glances at a picture on a shelf.)*

BILLY. She wasn't, like...*pretty*, huh? Mommy.

MACK. But what a sweetheart. Me, I never cared. I'd always got along good with plain women. Ma usedta' always say, there's a mystery inside every wallflower. Learn how to draw 'em out. I did.

BILLY. Yeah, what was Mommy's mystery?

MACK. More a dream than a mystery. At her age, she'd never expected to be a bride, let alone end up with family. But! Then! One rainy day, into the Broadway Nut Shop, aloooong comes –

BILLY. – Yeah, yeah, this loud guy who knew all about the history of licorice or somethin', and swept her off her feet. A guy who was younger, but not as smart as she was. Maybe Mommy's mystery was just that she was outta guys to pick from.

(Before startled **MACK** *replies:)*

BILLY. *(cont.)* – 'She want *me*?

MACK. 'Course Mommy *wanted* – What awful questions you're full of today!

BILLY. Or 'she just do it 'cause you pestered her to?

MACK. She wanted Daddy, too. Wasn't scrapin' the bottom of a darned barrel!

(moving off this)

All you are is dead tired. Eat some protein, peanut butter n'strawberry jam on B&B brown bread, get your head screwed on straight.

(nervously straightening up)

I'm run down, too. I got outta bed today, looked around here, seriously took stock of a few things.

BILLY. Yeah? *Really?*

MACK. Yessir, a real wake-up call. I realized, these tired old bunnies on our walls are way past their prime. They're pitiful, so darn faded. We need brand new ones, even if they don't quite make 'em like they used to.

BILLY. New *decorations?* That's what you think you and me need?

MACK. I know you picked these out by yourself. Oh, I remember when, too. Like it was yesterday. Mommy had to work late – what else was new – you'd come home all shook up about that bully in your fifth grade class – Anthony! The one his lunatic parents gave Dexedrine pills to, to calm him down! Anthony, the one who *murdered* the class pig –

BILLY. Guinea pi –

MACK. – With a chloroform-soaked sock puppet, wasn't it? They found his sick weapons in the dumpster behind PS 87. You'd fallen in love with the class pet. Afterwards, you crawled under your bed, to hide your tears from Daddy. But I knew what'd pick you up. So we went out to buy us all new decorations on seventy-second.

(BILLY has turned away, staring at decorations.)

MACK. *(cont.)* And that store's still *there*! So whatya say we do it again? Take down these ragged fellas, and put up brand new ones!

BILLY. Y'know, for, like…a halfa second…I actually thought –

(He stops.)

MACK. A halfa second…you thought what?

BILLY. I saw this movie, about a man 'got knocked in the head by a flyin' brick from, I dunno, a pizza oven explosion, and ended up with a whole new, like, personality. So for the last few days, I started to, like, *pretend*…that maybe that bump on the head you got… might change you.

MACK. Change me? How? Why on earth should I change?

(BILLY looks up at the decorations, shakes his head. **MACK** *panics:)*

What'd you think I was gonna tell you today? Billy? If you got somethin' to say, say it. What do I smell on your breath –

(He's trailing BILLY.)

BILLY. Stop followin' me like you gotta clip on my mittens!

MACK. Listen here, buster. The person who's gotta *change* 'round here isn't Daddy! You wanna walk out 'your smelly photocopy shop, fine! You don't need a bump on the head. You got your Daddy to back ya. So go for something *else*! See somethin' on the horizon for yourself. I've been hopin' you'd get up the gumption to thumb your nose at 'em.

BILLY. Such a expert on jobs.

MACK. You told me they talk about ya behind your back, laugh at ya –

BILLY. Laugh at *us*, Daddy. Ever since you came in to bring my *gloves* and hat.

MACK. Buncha lazy good-for-nothings nobody invited to these shores. We gotta getcha outta there. 'Wrong people 'round ya can ruin your whole perspective on life –

BILLY. Who are the right people? Our new "friends" in Red Bank? Is it really gonna be better there, Daddy? Huh? If there's anything there besides a empty Woolworths and a empty house 'smells like pee and reminds you of one you lived in for, like, twenty minutes, forty years ago, I'll go tonight!

MACK. 'Course there is –

BILLY. Wanna find out? How 'bout today. Let's walk around the whole town! For once, some street you never even been down before. With, like, *modern* buildings put up since 1980 or somethin'!

MACK. Today's no good for Red Bank, tomorrow's Easter –

BILLY. So? Like you always say, The Bunny handles Easter. Let's find out what's there, *now*, not leftover from when you were eight –

MACK. No –

BILLY. Why not? It's 'posed to be the place you wanna go back to, but you never want to spend any time there!

MACK. All this craziness is really about that *woman!* I didn't invite her, you did!

BILLY. But you're the one 'kept her here. Just so you could make sure she saw what a *wonderful* Daddy you are –

MACK. If you'd never found her to begin with, you'd be your old self!

BILLY. Yeah? Takin' a recharge day to watch you shuffle around, arrange your Libby's canned pumpkin you're proud to find, 'cause the label looks like something your Ma had in her pantry the day John Glenn flew in space?

MACK. So you found out that miserable woman isn't so fulla questions about ya. So? She's not your Mommy. Your Mommy died –

BILLY. I don't need a Mommy! I don't need new friends in Red Bank, and I don't need –

(He stops, before he says "you." **MACK** *panics:)*

MACK. All you need is to get back on track. Have yourself some fun! We'll go down to the docks. Watch some big gleaming liner come in from Europe. There's one due today, I checked! From Portugal! It's so warm for Easter Eve…I'll pack us up pimento cheese sandwiches, and we'll get ice cold root beers, and you can take a sketch pad and draw the ship, 'way you used to!

*(***BILLY** *stalks off, slams his door.)*

If you got alcohol in there, Daddy's beggin' you: Please don't drink it.

BILLY. *(off)* Go buy your new cardboard bunnies n'leave me alone.

*(***MACK** *goes to the window. He lets the sun shine on him for a long moment, then closes his eyes, pulls the drapes; the room darkens.)*

(He goes to a shelf, takes down a child's Easter basket. He puts it on the table, then takes out a new plastic bag of plastic "grass." He arranges it in the basket, then stops, just holds it. Lights fade.)

(Music: A vintage religious performance booms forth, Tennessee Ernie Ford and a chorus singing "Christ The Lord Has Risen Today" wafts in.* Then lights slowly rise again on:)

*See Music Use Note on Page 3

7.

*(The next day. The room's empty. The Easter basket has since been filled with candy, and is adorned with a bright new ribbon. A small new stuffed bunny sits next to it. Sound: doorbell. Then breathless **MACK** races in, just finishing making tea as he heads toward the door. He stops to turn off the hymn on the radio.)*

MACK. Cooooooming!

*(He opens on a visibly on-edge **ADELA**. She wears the same suit with a different blouse.)*

Well! You're so prompt. Himself was already gone when I dragged outta bed. But it's Easter. 'Means a lot to the both of us. He'll be back.

ADELA. 'Gone to one of them sunrise services?

MACK. Oh no. We don't do that, 'much as I love a pretty stained glass window, and cry at organ music. We tried the cranky Unitarians, so Billy could sing in a children's choir, play-act a shepherd. But the so-called "minister" calls God "She," likes *other* girls, and tells ya who to vote for for Mayor. Oh boy, we made *quite* a dramatic exit from one of their so-called "services," lemme tell ya.

(hanging up her coat)

Problems? Finding your way back?

ADELA. Once I 'done something, I can do it again. 'All looks different in daytime, but I could tell the taxicab driver just where to slow down.

MACK. You're lucky he understood ya.

ADELA. First I thought he was a Irish fellow, what with his red hair and freckles. But his name on the license had all these v's and z's in it.

MACK. How observant.

ADELA. Mr. Doyle says I got one a'those photographic minds.

MACK. In your line of work that's useful. What's your line again?

ADELA. Secretary to the Director of Administrative Services.

MACK. Ah! I smell some prestige.

ADELA. We're a team.

MACK. Now, now don't sell yourself short, Dear –

ADELA. We're only as strong as a Department as each of us is individually, Mr. Doyle says.

MACK. Sit, sit, take a load off. I made a pot of tea.

ADELA. Not one of them herbals, is it?

MACK. Good ol' Mister Lipton's. With Flow-Through tea bags.

ADELA. Mr. Doyle told me how in the armed services, if you drink too much made from a herb, and you get a drug test, they can think you take cocaine.

MACK. My, this Doyle fellow's quite an…influence, hm?

ADELA. He give me a chance when nobody else would.

MACK. 'Kind of mentor, was he? Have a Easter cookie. I had to go to three stores to find those.

ADELA. There were these other candidates for my job who'd applied when I did, who were rated higher n'me, who typed faster, and some had a nicer way of speaking on the phone. Or prettier clothes or nicer complexions. But he picked me.

MACK. For your photographic memory? – Have a cookie, Dear.

ADELA. Just because he had this feeling.

MACK. About your potential? Saw some drive, did he?

ADELA. It was 'cause I was s' average. He said he got *his* big break once 'cause somebody told him the average kind of person like him and like me gets ignored. If you're one of those people who don't ever stand out in a crowd, you need a helpin' hand so's you don't end up invisible.

MACK. His instincts paid off? You've done this Doyle proud?

ADELA. 'Guess so, I've won eleven awards for my employee suggestions.

MACK. My, my. What's an employee suggest nowadays?

ADELA. Form Revision's my specialty. Lotsa in-house forms have way too many boxes on 'em. Nobody really needs to know stuff that just disappears into the agency data base. I write up ways to cut 'em down to size. One form on supply requisition went from two whole pages to less than a half. I won the *"Liberty Bell" Fraud, Waste and Mismanagement Award* two years in a row for saving so much paper.

MACK. The Liberty Be – ?

ADELA. You get a silver-plated bell with your name on it. They have a luncheon over at the Mayflower Hotel. The first year they give us chrysanthemum corsages, but not the second. 'Next day, Mr. Doyle had a big bowl of flowers on my desk that come from his own back yard in Rockville.

MACK. My, you're not "invisible" at all. Poor Doyle couldn't function without you. You're headin' home tonight? Easter Monday used to be a holiday, but I bet Mr. Doyle has something *else* on tomorrow's calendar. *"Adela! Back! Today!"*

ADELA. I put it there m'self. You yourself don't have a job, do you?

MACK. *(ignoring this)* 'Mr. Doyle know much about you of a *personal* nature?

(**ADELA** *nervously nibbles a cookie.*)

ADELA. He knows I swell up when I get stung by a bee.

MACK. Useful.

ADELA. I told him I'd like to have a computer, so he gave me his old home one when he got a new model. I couldn't find nothing in the regs against it, since it wasn't a new gift. He keeps tellin' me not to be scared to assert m'self. So I try to. That's how come I...I wrote back to that boy.

MACK. And does your beloved Doyle...*know*? About Billy?

ADELA. *Billy*. Why would he know 'bout him. Nobody knows.

MACK. And you'd pretty much stopped thinking about Billy yourself, hm?

(She stares, suddenly steely. They both regroup.)

ADELA. This place a'yours has a sickly sweet smell. Like a whole buncha old vanilla extract bottles that never got thrown out.

(tension)

How's come you invited me back? I pretty much thought we was through.

MACK. I'm frankly surprised I had to call you. First. Dear, don'tcha wanna...*fix*...what happened?

*(***ADELA*** moves off; no answer.)*

That son of mine got the crazy idea that you don't want to know about him. How can that be? Your success with – what was it? – "form revision" – has gotta be based on some kinda curiosity.

(She throws down her cookie.)

ADELA. You ask me back here, just to get ugly? 'Cause I halfway guessed you might, and almost didn't come. I only did cause you seemed like a nice enough man. A smart man. 'Way you knew stuff about Christians stealin' Easter from the heathens n'all.

MACK. You were hangin' on my every word. Aren't you *as* curious about this child you've come all this way to see?

ADELA. I come here to *see* big ol' filthy New York. That boy just happens to live in it. It's a dern coincidence. Why 'you so interested in what I think, anyways? *Now?*

MACK. 'Scuse me –

ADELA. – 'Scuse *me*, but why do I haveta be as derned nosy as you?

MACK. Dear, when Billy found you in his computer, you didn't have to write back. You musta 'cause there were things you wanted to learn.

ADELA. What is it I'm 'posed to want to know about the boy? Whether he mixes his mushy peas n'carrots in with mashed potatoes before he eats 'em? Or gets sea sick on carnival rides? Or always wanted an aquarium that bubbles up in his bedroom? Or gets sad when he hears "I saw Mommy Kissin' Santy Claus?" When I marched into the lawyers' office to sign a messa' papers twenty years ago it was 'cause they promised me I didn't *have* to get "curious" about a derned thing.

MACK. So you can assert yourself after all.

ADELA. But there's things about *you*, Sir, I am kinda curious about. Like, what 'you *do*? Why don't you have no real job?

MACK. *(beat; eye contact)* My job is raising Billy.

ADELA. That boy isn't in no diapers no more.

MACK. Bein' a parent doesn't stop at high school.

ADELA. But he quit high school.

MACK. Billy didn't officially graduate 'cause he and I both needed time to grieve his mommy's untimely death.

ADELA. Died just before the ceremony, did she?

MACK. A few months before; how long doesn't matter –

ADELA. You kept the boy home from school all that time? What'd he do 'round here?

MACK. We took care of each other. We still do. A good parent never leaves his child's education up to others. Oh no, not in today's world. He takes charge. I held Billy back from kindergarten, 'cause he wasn't near ready.

ADELA. But you had yourself a Kindergarten right here. Looks like you still do.

(She finds herself drawn to the Easter basket.)

MACK. As a matter of fact, that was a magical time. I covered every sharp edge so he'd never bump his head. We had music, all day. Games –

ADELA. While your mizzuz went off to her office?

MACK. We all have our callings.

ADELA. Yours was bein' the mama.

MACK. The *daddy*.

ADELA. Most daddies go to work. Most daddies I seen –

MACK. – I worked, right here. Me. Not some tired senora wishin' she was home raisin' her *own* baby. Helping my son find his place in the world has been his Daddy's full-time job. Please leave that basket alone. Billy hasn't even seen it yet.

(She again eyes the basket, then **MACK**, *trying to connect the odd dots:)*

ADELA. What is it 'you're *doin'*, exactly, to put the boy on the road to his place in the world?

MACK. You're not getting a thing I'm talking about.

ADELA. I'll speak up when I don't get somethin'.

MACK. I believe I know a wee bit more about child rearing than you.

ADELA. That boy's a man. Still havin' a Easter basket?

MACK. Take that up with the Bunny.

ADELA. 'Beg your pardon?

MACK. The *Easter* Bunny? The person whose *biography* I impressed ya with last time? Maybe that's your problem. That big fella just never came to your house.

*(***ADELA*** looks at boxes,* **MACK**.*)*

ADELA. Why the two of y'all movin'? to a new town? Together. Now?

MACK. That *perfect* town holds a special place in my heart.

ADELA. Bill said everything's real *old* there. Includin' y'all's new house.

MACK. Exactly! There's a main street that's got its original Christmas decorations. A barber shop 'been there sixty-five years, with its original barber chairs intact. And until just this past week, one of the last remaining dime stores. A Woolworth's.

ADELA. *Woolworth's?*

(**MACK** *grabs a vintage post card from a lower shelf, waves it at her:*)

MACK. Once upon a time, a place...you could catch your breath.

ADELA. *(baffled)* A *dime* store?

MACK. *(beat)* At a quarter after four on a Saturday afternoon, 'third week of October. Air outside's nippy; sky, slate gray. Everywhere, it smells like burning leaves. You come inside Woolworth's, it hits you, a warm cloud of furnace air and talcum powder and sawdust and caramel popcorn. You sit on a vinyl-covered stool that needs oil, creaks real loud as you spin, 'til you get dizzy. Then you sip a vanilla coke at the black marble counter, served in a Dixie cup resting in an aluminum-plated holder. The lady next to you drinkin' her malt with a white gloved hand. Then you walk up and down aisle after aisle, stocked with model airplanes and... thread...and placemats with maps of New Jersey on 'em, and plastic catsup containers in the shape of big fat tomatoes and...and wooden hamburger presses, and a whistling clerk with a pencil behind his ear and a smile on his face is stackin' boxes of valentines, real neatly, real careful not to muss the embossed red velvet hearts on topa' each box.

ADELA. *(beat)* Valentines? In October?

MACK. In that *town*, it's as if...it's *always* October!

ADELA. Huh. If it's s'nice...why didn't y'all move there lots earlier?

MACK. Billy's Mommy shared some of your *confusion* about what's charming anymore. After her accident, he and I bought a bungalow, just two blocks from where I lived in fifth grade. We'll spend the resta our lives there.

ADELA. Is there work for Billy in this Red Bank?

MACK. There's a chance to be *contented* –

ADELA. What skills 'he gonna use in the work force? He good with numbers?

MACK. "Numbers," he's gifted with food. An award-winning baker. Maybe his achievement isn't up there with your eleven "employee suggestions," but he was a finalist in The Pillsbury Bake-off. Youngest contestant in the history of New York State. His interest started lots earlier. Billy *cooked* before he *walked*. He'd put all his stuffed animals around a toy table and serve them make-believe stew in plastic bowls.

ADELA. He didn't mention nothin' about baking to me. Maybe he's kinda embarrassed, 'cause he's a boy.

MACK. A *boy?*

ADELA. Coulda outgrowed it, when he gave up playin' house with doll babies.

MACK. What's more satisfying than cooking wonderful meals for people? Not everyone dreams of serving some Doyle 'til they get a gold watch or…or a silver liberty bell.

ADELA. To take a boy outta high school, just so's he can learn to bake bread –

MACK. My son had the good sense to finally throw in the towel at school 'cause he wasn't buyin' all the dog-eat-dog. And early on, I…only I!…could see there's a sweeter side to him that's too special, too…tender for just about every ugly thing on the other side of that door!

(The front door opens, **BILLY** *enters. Startled, he just stares at* **ADELA**, *then starts toward his room.* **ADELA** *calls out, taking a step closer.)*

ADELA. I…I just thought I'd – say 'bye. One more time. Since I'm up here.

BILLY. Another crummy idea.

ADELA. Wasn't mine! Your Daddy's! He called me, at the hotel.

*(***BILLY** *stops, jerks his head toward* **MACK**.*)*

MACK. You…you 'been miserable –

BILLY. Think it's all 'cause of her?

ADELA. Your daddy's been fillin' me in on lotsa things I didn't get 'round to askin'.

(BILLY turns on MACK, staggering a bit again.)

BILLY. You devil. Findin' the "mystery" inside another wallflower.

MACK. More alcohol. Have those nasty fellas in that copy shop been givin' you rum?

BILLY. What all's he been telling you?

ADELA. You never did mention how you almost won that big bakin' contest.

(Freshly thrown, BILLY glares at MACK.)

BILLY. *He* almost won it. All that man's ideas.

MACK. Now that was your recipe, Billy. Don't you be ashamed –

BILLY. You musta' made up the ingredients one of those long days when I was at school. I'd come home, there'd be heaps a' dirty laundry, Mommy would wonder what he'd been *doin'* all day –

MACK. We don't need to go into all –

BILLY. *(over)* – Besides listen to his Ma's old Doris Day records while he figured out which cereal box contest to enter. Or half painted the room another crayon color. She'd find stacks of *coupons* he'd, like, *hoard*, so he could wander round grocery stores.

MACK. Why don't you go take yourself a nice hot bath –

BILLY. – Y'know, people always did talk about you. Behind your back. It didn't *start* with the copy shop –

MACK. Billy –

BILLY. – Kids. Even *teachers*. 'Cause you wouldn't leave after ya dropped me off in the morning. You'd hang out, at first inside the school, 'til your loud voice started disturbin' people and the principal asked you to clear out –

MACK. William! That's enough, now –

BILLY. – But even then, ya wouldn't go! You'd peer in our windows with that big stupid grin. Later on, you always got to school to pick me up like, forty minutes early. Rain, sleet, snow, you'd be out there, carrying my slicker and umbrella, chattering away to the Jamaican nannies about where to buy the kinda old-fashioned galoshes like they made when you were a kid. Every once in a while, coupla' other dads might show, too. Who took the day off. In shirts n'*ties*, carrying *briefcases* and fold-up *computers*. But the one dad who *always* had the day *off* didn't ever speak to them –

MACK. My days weren't *off* –

BILLY. – You hung out with the babysitters. 'Used to bring them hot coffee or homemade lemonade in your rusty 1961 thermos.

MACK. You just need some food –

BILLY. Your answer to everything, hot soup, loaf of bread from the oven. But all that's just an excuse to finally get to some big old gooey treat. Then, remember? A "sur-*priiiiiise*," after dinner.

MACK. Billy, family traditions are private –

BILLY. You told me I was 'posed to *brag* to her. 'Bout *you*. "Daddy's got ya a surprise for after dinner!" Poor Mommy'd be locked in the bedroom, on the phone with, like, Tokyo. I'd be off taking my bath, still told I was too young to shower, right? Then I'd come in, there'd be some wrapped up thing, hidden. Something real useful when you're, like, *thirteen*. A stuffed Christmas *elf* with a note sayin' "Bet Billy's been a good boy this year!"

(*to* **ADELA**)

See that shelf fulla' junk up there? Most of it I got for the After Supper Surprise, even when I was too old to want any of it.

MACK. You always loved the countdown to Christmas; still do –

BILLY. – And whenever anything broke, *you're* the one who freaked…and fixed 'em with scotch tape or bandaids, to keep Mommy from throwin' 'em in the trash. Now you want to pack it up, move it to that house? For what?

MACK. We'll talk about all 'this if you want, when she's gone –

BILLY. To open a junk store? Where you can sell the Good Old Days to a buncha "new friends" along the Navasink river? Gonna fill that big ol' empty Woolworths with all *this* useless crap?!

(He smacks the wall near the shelving. A couple of items tremble. **ADELA** *sees a delicate Christmas ornament teeter. Fearing it's about to fall, she rushes over, preemptively rescuing it. She holds it very carefully. Sense of wonder:)*

ADELA. I never had one a'these. 'Cause Quakers think decorations turn the birth of the Lord into a false idol.

*(***BILLY*** wheels around:)*

BILLY. Huh – ?! That means *I'm* a Quaker?

ADELA. Like y'all I'm nothin', now. We called ourselves "The Friends" back when I was one. We never had pretty stuff like this 'round, but this big family 'cross the street did. They made paper chains at Christmas and strung popcorn and cranberries to put on a pine tree the daddy dug up hisself from some farm out near Middleburg. They had this record of chipmunks singin' about Christmastime not bein' late. When somebody told me it was just a regular buncha grown-up singers, played at a fast speed to make the voice sound all squeaky thataways, I didn't believe 'em. I wanted to think there actually were these chipmunks who had 'emselves a chipmunk Christmas. I was little, I didn't know chipmunks couldn't talk, let alone sing about Christmas or any other thing. I think I cried, finding out. The family invited me to go to their church one Christmas eve, and I was gonna. I'd one time snuck into a church, and hid in back, and seen all these satin shelves of candles. The Friends meetin's just take place in a basement, so the candles were what I wanted to see again. But Quakers are afraid of Catholics, and when Mama found out, she locked me in my room. I got so mad, I banged on the door, and when she ignored me, just using my fists, I started usin' my head, to make me a bigger sound, pounding and pounding. My forehead got bruised and on Christmas morning, when we went to the Friends meeting, I looked like I'd been beat to a pulp, and my ears started ringing. Truth is, I'd done it to myself. I still got a dent up here, from that, and every now n'then my ears still ring. They rang the other night, after I left here.

(to BILLY)

ADELA. *(cont.)* The daddy in the family sometimes gave me "surprises," too. Even though Mama wouldn't let me keep 'em, that was okay. Only time I really liked toys was in stores. In boxes. With clear cellophane over the faces of the dolls or what-have-you. Toys kept way up, on a high shelf, so the cellophane didn't even have fingerprints on it.

BILLY. 'Must be why you gave away that doll you won.

ADELA. Sometimes I wish I'd known a child to give it to, and that I coulda watched her play with it. But children are s'loud and move too fast and make me nervous.

(MACK picks up a couple of dropped toys, keeps watching BILLY.)

BILLY. 'Wish I'd given mine away. I'm not moving those old toys to Red Bank. Not movin' *me* there either.

MACK. What? 'Course ya are –

BILLY. You're the fool 'wants to die there, not me.

MACK. Live there. Both of us. Nobody else's gonna die for a long time.

ADELA. You'd just stay on here instead?

MACK. Oh no. You haven't thrown out a pop bottle or picked up a sneaker in twenty years. You'd be buried alive in trash in a week.

BILLY. *(wave of hand toward shelving)* Once we unpack in Red Bank, I'll be buried alive under *this*.

MACK. Let's take her to her hotel! Then you and me take a walk in the park –

BILLY. Ride the merry-go-round? Name our horses? Uh-uh –

MACK. You just need to quit that job! That's what's causin' all this! Quit! Then you'll think straight!

ADELA. *(trying to piece this together)* Don't one of ya'll have to work, just to earn your keep?

BILLY. One of us? What would Daddy do? Be a clown at kids' parties? He'd love the costume, yeah, bells on a hat –

MACK. William –

BILLY. – Hey! Or how 'bout Santa at Macys?! Buncha kids linin' up to sit in his lap. But it might get him down, see, since they'd get freaked when he started shouting about how Lionel Trains aren't like they were in 1959.

MACK. All this is alcohol talkin', not my Billy –

BILLY. Lucky for him, though, a job would be, like, a luxury. That fallin' down dream house in Red Bank doesn't have a mortgage. We got to pay cash, 'cause when my hard-workin' banker mom got knocked in front of a subway car, it set *this* guy up, for the resta his life. Sometimes, I seriously wonder if she *jumped*, just to get free.

(MACK suddenly lashes out, smacking BILLY on the side of the head, hard. This is momentous, since he's never done anything like this before. ADELA covers her ears. BILLY isn't hurt, but he's stunned and loses his balance, falling back, knocking the Easter basket and toy rabbit to the floor. The candy spills. BILLY cowers, shocked. A small bottle of rum falls out of his jacket. MACK picks it up. No one moves.)

MACK. You got a few more interesting memories you could share with her 'fore she heads back to Ol' Virginie. 'Bout stuff *not* up there on our shelves. Things that weren't all wrapped up in shiny paper and called surprises. Ya could show off the yarmulke you stole from that shop on Broadway, n'hid from me. You didn't wanna be Catholic like her, but for a long time you pretended to be Jewish, remember? After you got caught neckin' with that rich Orthodox girl, some psychologist calls me in and says that was one of a whole buncha lies you'd told, 'cause you got some *identity* rigmarole. But I just told em to mind their own beeswax, 'cause you'd always had a big imagination. A kid who staged an Olympics for all the toys he loved.

(He waves at the shelves. **BILLY** *grabs the bottle back, takes a pull, drops it empty to the floor.)*

You could also show her that piece of cut up bedding you sleep with. Tell her how ya never stopped suckin' your thumb even after Mommy warned you'd get buck teeth like a hillbilly. You could tell her how you tried to have sleepovers with your little friends, but got *caught*, when those two fellas woke up and found you curled up with that red, gnawed-on thumb shoved in your mouth, and made fun. Stick out your hand, show her how that thumb's still raw to this very day. Tell her how, even now, ya still got that piece of baby bedspread under your bed, and reach down, and grab up a handful of filthy fuzz every night. Tell her how one time I came in and caught you with it, and you hid in a corner, and I said "No big deal, it's fine with Daddy." I'd known that ratty thing had been there for years, and I told ya, suck your thumb 'til you're forty if that's what it takes for ya to feel good in this world.

BILLY. Why didn't you just yank it outta my hand and throw it away?

(This simple truth hangs in the air.)

ADELA. 'Night the baby come, when pains started, I hid in a corner, too. I tried to stop 'em. Tried to pretend there weren't no pains. I still couldn't believe it was happenin' to me. 'Whole time I carried it, locked up by Mama, I thought, all this will just go away some day. I'll go back, and graduate, and things'll be like they was.

BILLY. I was *the* baby.

ADELA. I thought, I'll run across the street to be with that family like I always did. They'd got 'em a brand new puppy. Big thing. The daddy'd said it was half wolf, and I believed him. But I hadn't even played with it, once, since I'd gotten too big to go out without everybody knowin'. I watched their wolf puppy out my window. It was muddy all the time, they didn't take real good care of it, didn't buy it a collar or get it rabies shots. Locked it outside in the pourin' rain and it yapped 'til it was plumb hoarse. Half wolf or not, he was a loyal thing. But it chased cars and one time got somethin' chemical-like sprayed up in its lil' eyes. The daddy of this family did things his way, and didn't believe in payin' no vets, so they didn't do nothin' and the dog was half-blind after that, used to run smack into walls. Still... they never got rid of *him*.

BILLY. Who was "the baby's" daddy? Who got you pregnant?

ADELA. *(a firm shake of her head)* Uh-*uh*.

BILLY. Who?!

ADELA. *No.* I was scared the whole time in the restaurant that you'd get around to that. But no, Sir. It's just not polite a'you to ask me.

BILLY. Not – Not *polite?*! Was it...Mr. Warren Patterson Doyle?

ADELA. I didn't know Mr. Doyle when I was sixteen. And he'd never do somethin' like that.

BILLY. Then was it the daddy in the family with the chipmunk songs? Huh?! Was I the "surprise" he gave ya?! You came all this way! Just...tell me...*something!* Who was it?! Who –

(**ADELA** *has continued to shake her head, holding firm. In her face, a cry from his soul:*)

WHO...AM I?!

(*Cornered* **ADELA** *just looks at* **MACK**, *her emotions coming to the surface. A revelation, and a gift:*)

ADELA. His son. That's who you are.

BILLY. Whatya mean *his?*

ADELA. *His.* Him.

(MACK turns toward her, unexpectedly startled by her validation.)

Right here is your only real daddy.

(She glances at a dusty Santa mask, then at MACK:)

I think he's wrong 'bout one thing, though. You might turn out to be a right good Santy Claus. As Mr. Doyle says, there's always a place for us average people in this world.

(She appreciatively takes in the shelves, again, turns to rocked BILLY:)

If I was you, I wouldn't throw out any of these.

(Her eyes fall on the bunny on the floor, next to the basket. She picks it up, starts to put it on the shelf, but stops, cradles the toy; for the first time, her face breaks into a childlike smile. BILLY glances over.)

BILLY. Keep it.

MACK. Maybe he brought it for you.

(ADELA picks up her coat, and, still holding the toy bunny like a treasure, quietly heads toward the door. MACK opens it for her. ADELA looks around the room, then back at MACK. MACK nods – perfunctorily, but a silent acknowledgement of something ineffable.)

(She leaves. BILLY stands. Pensive MACK turns to BILLY, picking up a dropped thread from the confrontation, though not defensively:)

MACK. What did I do, when you were at school? Mostly, just waited, 'til the best part of my day. When you got home. That's why, when you hit ninth grade, I wanted to start over.

BILLY. Get a job?

MACK. Get a brand new little brother or sister for you.

BILLY. Another baby? *Then?*

MACK. Me, I woulda been happy as a clam to do it all over again. We coulda dusted off your old crib in the basement, put it back in our room. Eventually, I planned on gettin' bunk beds for the two of you. But, Mommy said she'd barely had enough time with you, and we were both too old. Now, Mommy's g*one*. Many a night since, I've laid awake, wishin' I'd put my foot down.

(Reeling – momentarily oddly jealous – **BILLY** *looks down at the Coney Island bear, clad in his baby clothes, starts toward the door.)*

MACK. Where 'you going now?

BILLY. Buy a newspaper again. Look for a new job.

MACK. *(grabbing, from shelf:)* Why don't you finally fill out your cooking academy application! Honest, they don't give a darn 'ya just got your GED. Come on, get started. I'll keep ya company! In fact! What *I* oughta do? Finally seal those boxes with masking tape and hide 'em, so I keep my darned hands off 'em, and I'm not tempted to take anything out again. Dare me to?

*(***BILLY** *shoves the application back:)*

BILLY. I don't *want* to.

(beat; a realization:)

And *you* don't really wanna live in that house. You didn't wanna call the cops the day we found out about kids breakin' in. When I asked 'em to patrol, you got all weirded out. 'Cause I think, like, deep down, you hope somebody'll go in and burn the place down. And then you won't *have* to move. You're scared to, Daddy.

(Hit, **MACK** *doesn't answer.)*

But *I'm* scared…stayin' *here*. I can't stay here.

MACK. Where else could you go? All by yourself?

BILLY. Maybe just…outside to play by *myself*. Like everybody else.

(silence)

MACK. "Go." Wish I could just "go" to bed like Rip Van Winkle. Sleep straight through till October. If it was October, things'd be easier somehow.

(BILLY's eyes fall on the scattered Easter basket:)

BILLY. But you love Easter.

(BILLY bends down, picks up candy, puts it back in the basket. He's suddenly gripped with intense contradictory feelings, nostalgic, yet sensing an opportunity for long-delayed escape. BILLY takes a candy egg, unwraps the foil, pops it in his mouth)

That bunny never forgets, huh?

(MACK puts the dropped rum bottle on the table next to the basket.)

MACK. Our Easter supper's simple. I got some of your favorites, even if they don't exactly add up to a holiday meal. Meat loaf, those duchess potatoes from the frozen section. You can make your gravy. Y'know, I think I packed our gravy boat, 'one usedta be my Ma's? All chipped anyway, I should throw it out.

(beat)

Whenever *we* moved, my own Ma and me, each time, I got homesick. The kinda homesick where it actually hurts. Homesick for wherever we just left. No matter how mean the kids had been, or how noisy it'd been outside my window. Or how temporary.

BILLY. You never told me that.

MACK. I never told ya plenty.

(beat)

Why didn't I get to know other dads at your school? I never thought they had a darned thing I wanted.

(shrug)

MACK. *(cont.)* Jobs. My own ma had a hundred. Hated 'em all. To me, the babysitters got to have fun.

BILLY. *(surveying moving detritus)* Daddy. Don't do any more boxes. No more packing.

(BILLY turns, finishes righting the basket, then picks it up, puts it up on the shelf next to the countless toys. MACK suddenly goes to BILLY, and throws his arms around him.)

MACK. I thought you were gonna go with her! I thought she'd trick ya! And you'd fall for her tricks, and I'd *lose* ya – to *her*! Somehow, 'seemed easier to think of givin' you back than…than watchin' ya just – just disappear. Into thin air.

(beat)

Oh Billy. I know – it's *time*. The day I 'been dreadin' since that train trip home with ya, when you were three weeks old!

(MACK clings to his son. Then finally breaks the embrace, pulling away, without a trace of self-pity.)

(At the door BILLY holds, glances at the wall, as if looking for something among its disparate collected belongings that he's somehow missed.)

(MACK turns to the shelving as well, reaches up, locates a crudely made Santa beard, balls of cotton glued to cut out paper. He blows off some of the dust, holds it up to his face, chuckling. Then affixes it to himself with the attached rubber bands.)

(BILLY smiles nervously, instinctively taking a step into the room. But as he silently realizes this is a moment he can't turn back from, he wills himself toward the open door. And exits.)

(Once alone, MACK picks up the stuffed teddy bear wearing BILLY's baby clothes, then sits, places it on his lap, as if it's a small child.)

MACK. HO! HO! HO! Oh no, what's this?! Don't you cry, son. 'Nothing to be scared of. Look! There's your Daddy! Right over there, see? Your *Daddy* wouldn't *leave* you…

(As **MACK** *adjusts the "child" on his lap, sounds from the window: children playing below. The children's voices get louder, then disappear in the distance. There's a sudden stillness. It visibly grips* **MACK**. *But rather than dissolve, he places the teddy bear on the chair, and makes a decision: he slips* **BILLY**'s *baby clothing off of it.)*

(Stripped of toddler apparel...it's suddenly just an old toy again. **MACK** *tosses the clothes on top of one of the packing boxes, almost indifferently. Then stares at the toy. Even in his heartbreak, all of this somehow feels like overdue relief.)*

(He smiles at the toy, wistfully, to be sure. Then stands, rips off the Santa mask. As he tosses it in the trash, and it lands with finality, the lights fade...

...Ending the play.)

COSTUME PLOT

ACT ONE

1.
MACK
Purple long-sleeved sports shirt
Light brown pleated corduroy slacks
Tan cardigan
Vintage wool pea coat
Distressed men's figure skates
Scuffed brown leather tie shoes
Brightly colored scarf/muffler
Wool mittens
Dark socks

BILLY
Pastel long-sleeved polo shirt
Dark green hooded wool car coat
Baggy jeans, rolled up cuffs
Multi-colored knit hat with pom-pom
Matching scarf
Converse high-top sneakers, white socks

2.
MACK
Same corduroy slacks
Gray undershirt (under scene 1)
Dark wool or flannel bathrobe
Distressed leather slippers

BILLY
Same jeans, same sneakers
Black long-sleeved undershirt (under scene 1)
Gray short-sleeved polo shirt (rain-dampened)
Wet hair

3.
MACK
Same corduroy slacks, socks, shoes (scene 1)
Red checkered shirt (over same gray undershirt)
Corduroy jacket with suede elbow patches
Black felt beret

BILLY
Same jeans, sneakers, black undershirt
Remove polo shirt, tuck undershirt
Add: faded cotton spring jacket

4.
MACK
L.L. Bean-styled flannel nightshirt
Wool socks

BILLY
Cotton pajamas
Same white socks

Mid-scene quick change to:
Pleated (new) khaki slacks
Pink (new) long-sleeved cotton shirt
Light cobalt blue (new) cotton vest
Plaid clip-on bow tie
Same sneakers

Add: wool car coat, knit hat (scene 1)

5.
BILLY
Same

ADELA
Ecru linen pantsuit with tailored jacket
Off-white high-necked cotton blouse
Pale silk scarf
Tan trench coat
Brown leather shoulder bag
Beige flats or pumps with low heels

MACK
Brown corduroy slacks
Rubber galoshes or rain boots
Wool plaid long-sleeved shirt
Burgundy sweater vest with " Dad" buttons (see properties)
Hooded/lined winter parka (snow-dampened)
Scarf, mittens (scene 1)

ACT TWO

6.
MACK
Vintage chenille or heavy cotton bathrobe
Striped summer pajamas
Slippers (scene 2)

BILLY
Duplicate/same khaki slacks, wrinkled
Duplicate/same shirt, wrinkled, worn out
Remove: vest, bow tie, shoes, socks

7.
MACK
Dark green corduroy slacks
Solid yellow or lilac shirt
Tan cardigan (scene 1; optional)
String tie, knotted with ceramic Easter basket clasp (optional)
Same slippers

ADELA
Same pantsuit, shoes, coat
Change to: pale gray silk blouse

BILLY
Black jeans
Black undershirt (scenes 2, 3)
Gray hooded "Hoodie" sweatshirt-jacket
Sneakers, untied; no socks
Dampened hair slicked back/re-combed

PROPERTIES PLOT
ACT ONE

1.

2 stacked breakfast dishes/2 juice glasses (dining table)
Pile of clean/folded bath towels (sideboard/table)
3-4 cardboard cartons (semi-packed with books)
Wrapped cherry popsicle
Distressed figure skates, laced together (Billy's)
Bag of blue corn chips, opened
Kitchen glass of milk
Chinese Checkers (sideboard)

2.

Distressed vintage version of Scrabble
Culinary Institute multi-page application
Desk drawer key

3.

Shopping bags (filled, Woolworth's purchases)
Boxed air filters
3-4 Halloween figure candles

4.

Dinner plate with jam-filled muffins
Coffee mug adorned with "DAD"
Glass of milk
Wooden serving tray
2 cardboard cartons (semi-filled, keepsakes/books)
Stack of childhood snapshots
Larger photo of Billy (age 12, posed in Chef's toque)
Paper "Happy Easter" decorations
Large Gap shopping bag (filled, duplicate khakis)
Pocket comb (Mack's pocket)
Metal lock box
Cash (5 twenties atop stack of fake bills)
5-6 New York restaurant menus clipped together as souvenirs
Distressed backpack (Billy)

5.

Restaurant "doggie bag" (foil-wrapped contents unseen)
Additional paper Easter decorations
Bottled "Snapple"-style iced tea
Jelly glass adorned with cartoon figures

Large framed photo of Red Bank house (see Setting notes)
2 grocery bags (filled, snow-dampened)
8-10 "World's Best Dad"/"#1 Dad" buttons/ribbons (Mack's vest)
Ovaltine
Bag of miniature marshmallows, sealed
Miscellaneous groceries, boxed/can goods
Child's animal-themed umbrella
4 3 x 5 handwritten note cards, clipped together (Adela's purse)
Frosted grocery-store Easter sheet cake (or iced foam rubber)

ACT TWO

6.
Large stuffed bear (Coney Island prize)
Toddler's matching shorts and tank top (on bear)
2 children's mugs
Wooden serving tray (scene 4)
China teapot filled with cocoa
Bag of miniature marshmallows, opened
Easter basket (empty)
Easter basket plastic "grass"

7.
Add to basket: purple bow
Add to basket: candy*
Small stuffed rabbit*
Heirloom tea pot
Matching tea cups
Dinner plate with iced Easter cookies
Same tray (scene 6)
Vintage Woolworth's postcard
Delicate glass/crystal Christmas ornament
Pint-sized rum bottle
Culinary Institute application (scene 2)
Homemade cotton Santa beard/partial mask

*Note on basket contents: Though composed of classics, i.e. jelly beans, Cadbury eggs and foil-wrapped holiday treats, popular teen candies are prominent, too, maybe packages of Billy's favorites (Twizzlers, mints, gum). The stuffed rabbit should be a real or faux Steiff rather than a pastel bunny. These items reveal how Mack keeps Easter traditions alive, always consciously updated, rather than a delusional assumption that Billy holds onto the narrow tastes or responses of a young child.

THE SETTING

Mack and Billy's apartment is a New York City pre-war. If its "bones" – vintage high ceilings and other architecture detailing – might be coveted in the real estate market, its minimal updates reveal middle-class occupants with a modest lifestyle. The playing area is the combined living/dining room. Its character-chosen set dressings (detailed below) provide distinctive ambiance, but a simple ground plan will work. On the upstage wall a doorway or arch leads to a hallway and bedrooms. Adjacent is an alcove leading to an off-stage front door, with visible coat hooks holding hats, scarves, backpacks. On the downstage right wall is a window with blinds or drapes. On the opposite wall by the dining area a downstage left (if possible, swinging) doorway leads to a kitchen. The cozy furnishings include: a wooden table seating three with matching chairs; a loveseat behind a small coffee table; a sideboard with an older model radio and a 70's era stereo system; and in front of the down right window, a multi-drawer desk with Billy's computer.

The apartment is on the dark side and as noted, its walls are painted in saturated colors. The effect can be startling but must not suggest strategic interior decoration or department store window preciousness. And though chock full of twenty years of memorabilia, the rooms are not cramped. Mack has clearly resisted a garage sale purge of accumulated belongings but keeps things clean and even neat. All tables and surfaces are utilitarian. Despite the stalled packing and delayed chores in the first scene, a sense of an underlying, family-sustaining order prevails — one based on a deep respect for domestic ritual. The set must not in any way suggest that Mack is a pathological hoarder. The shelves are laden but not a secret stockpile of eccentric possessions. Current moving crisis aside, this is a fully functioning home maintained by a mostly practical man.

Accordingly, the wall-lined bookshelves vividly celebrate a happy past and beloved traditions, holding miscellaneous keepsakes, holiday items and many framed photos of Billy, toddler through teen (with both Mack and Billy's late mother). The mix of toys should be eclectic, still-used board games prominent, and a combo of folkloric/fairy tale figures and a sprinkling of pop culture. Familiar items — say, identifiable characters from Disney or PBS — should neither be excluded nor draw undue attention. Mack's reverence for childhood's magic is his de facto religion. Rather than censor or discriminate against its diverse icons, he has sought to be inclusive.

His grousing aside, Mack is not really a Luddite. If he clings to a turntable and his vinyl recordings, he grudgingly watches TV (as Billy notes, with decidedly retro preferences). But Billy's computer is a real threat to his father, a gleaming, intimidating presence. Whenever its glowing screen casts a grayish white light, it provides a portal on an encroaching world, one Mack's apartment window cannot reveal. Finally, in strong contrast, is the framed photograph of the unoccupied Red Bank home. Looming large over all proceedings and shot against a pristine October sky, it's nevertheless a kind of haunted house, as much a threat as an idyllic promise to both men.

**Also by
Hal Corley...**

ODD

Mama and Jack Carew

Please visit our website **samuelfrench.com** for complete descriptions and licensing information

www.ingramcontent.com/pod-product-compliance
Lightning Source LLC
Chambersburg PA
CBHW070647300426
44111CB00013B/2308